CW00548164

A LITTLE]
AROUND TH.
SOUTH WEST COAST PATH

Joy Gower

ARTHUR H. STOCKWELL LTD
Torrs Park, Ilfracombe, Devon, EX34 8BA
Established 1898
www.ahstockwell.co.uk

British Library Cataloguing-in-Publication Data.
A catalogue record for this book is available
from the British Library.

Arthur H. Stockwell Ltd bears no responsibility
for the accuracy of information recorded in this book.

ISBN 978-0-7223-5068-3
Printed in Great Britain by
Arthur H. Stockwell Ltd
Torrs Park   Ilfracombe
Devon EX34 8BA

INTRODUCTION

I completed the last section of the 630-mile South West Coast Path one month before my eighty-fourth birthday, having walked 353 miles on my own and 277 miles with friends.

It all began when I and fifteen other walkers – mainly strangers – walked the first section of the path (Minehead to Combe Martin) as part of the Exmoor Walking Festival. At the end of the holiday six or so of us decided to continue walking the path – and it became addictive! We planned to walk two weekends a year.

For various reasons, there were several sections I was unable to walk with them and regretfully I had to drop out due to a knee problem when we reached Clovelly.

By the time the knee problem was solved, my walking friends had reached Padstow, so I had a decision to make – I could begin again at Padstow and always regret not completing the path or I could walk the sections I had missed on my own and catch them up.

So, walking on my own and using my camper van, I caught them up at Padstow and walked with them as far as the Helford river. At that point I decided to walk the rest of the coast path on my own, in my own time.

My friends carried on and completed their walk in 2015 and I joined them for their last section – and to help them celebrate!

I continued to plod on at my own pace, to complete the path.

I had walked the Dorset section (approximately eighty-five miles) to celebrate my eightieth birthday year. I also walked the

3

alternative inland route (West Bexington to Osmington Mills along the South Dorset Ridgway) in two parts (seventeen miles) a couple of years ago.

I wouldn't have missed walking the beautiful South West Coast Path for all the world, not only for the magnificent scenery, carpets of violets and primroses, bluebell woods, seals basking on the rocks, etc., etc., but also for the friends I have made.

Dream it – believe it – achieve it! It starts with one single step!

Me taking a breather on a hot day at a war memorial
on the coast path between Polperro and Talland.

The beach at Perranporth.

The eighteen-mile Chesil Beach (usually called Chesil Bank). It consists of pebbles, which are larger at the Portland end.

Chalk cliffs on the Dorset section of the coast path.

THE SOUTH WEST COAST PATH

Minehead to Porlock Weir

Date: 5 May 2008
Distance: 9.5 miles
Weather: fantastic!
Leader: Antony

We were a group of fifteen walkers staying at the Yarn Market Hotel in Dunster, near Minehead, Somerset.

We were setting out only to walk the Exmoor section of the South West Coast Path, being the thirty-five miles from Minehead to Combe Martin.

It was the first time that it had been included in the Exmoor Walking Festival – so we were the guinea pigs! Little did we know that for about six of us walking the coast path would become an addiction!

Our leader was Antony, the owner of the Yarn Market Hotel.

Our walk actually started from the hotel in Dunster, due to our minibus being vandalised, thus making our first walk twelve miles, instead of nine and a half miles. What a good start! It was sunny and hot with a cloudless blue sky. We walked via Dunster Beach, stopping for a group photograph at the official start of the walk near Minehead Harbour.

From that point it was up, up, up for about two miles – up steps, through woodland and over heathland, seeing Exmoor ponies,

7

brilliant-yellow gorse and beautiful coastal views.

Just as I was thinking I couldn't go another step, and longing for a break, there was Penny, a valued member of staff from the Yarn Market Hotel, with a small minibus serving coffee, tea and biscuits! What a lifesaver!

We later had a picnic lunch near Selworthy Beacon, enjoying the coastal views before we made our way down the steep and rough path to the beach of Porlock Bay at Bossington, and on to the bank of the pebble beach.

Unfortunately the tide was coming in fast! I have a very interesting photograph of the walkers wading through the water! Since we walked that section that year, it has been decided to let nature take its course at that point, and there is now a slight diversion.

We had been looking forward to enjoying an ice cream at the end of our walk, but, due to our walk being twelve miles instead of the nine and a half miles, yes, the shop was closed!

We all agreed it had been a great day!

Porlock Weir to Foreland Lighthouse

Date: 6 May 2008
Distance: 10 miles
Leader: Keith

After such a great day the previous day, we were looking forward to another day of coastal views.

The minibus took us to Porlock Weir, where the walk started with a steep climb from the harbour up steps and narrow paths into beautiful woods made up of mixed trees, rhododendrons and other shrubs, bluebells and a few late-flowering primroses. The path was very undulating, sometimes leading us up and down steps, and over plank bridges across streams, etc.

In the middle of the wood we found the little Culbone Church, said to be one of the smallest churches in England, with its tiny spire. Culbone Church is thirty-five feet long, with a twelve-foot-eight-inches-wide nave. It has no electric lighting and it seats about thirty people. Services are still held at the church, which is dedicated to St Bueno. We had just left the church when – who was this coming to meet us? Antony and two of his staff carrying urns of coffee and tea and biscuits! What a champion! We were so deep in the woods they had to leave the minibus and walk! Antony and his hotel staff really do go the extra mile!

Views, even though we were overlooking the sea, were limited because of the heat mist. It could have been worse – it could have been raining!

Before we set out it was decided we would end the day *before* the lighthouse, doing the remainder of the walk the next day, making it a ten-mile walk instead of 12.3 miles. Unfortunately this meant climbing a very steep hill to meet up with the minibus. It nearly proved one hill too many for all of us!

Culbone Church.

few views. A few months later I walked it on my own. Leaving my camper van at Hunter's Inn, I set out to walk to Combe Martin in perfect weather under a cloudless blue sky.

There were fantastic clear views to the Welsh coast once I had climbed the steep hill from Hunter's Inn. Then I carried on to Great Hangman and Little Hangman before dropping steeply down into Combe Martin. There were surprisingly few walkers about for such a glorious day, until I reached Little Hangman nearing the end of the walk.

When I reached Combe Martin I had a choice to make – either to retrace my steps to my camper van parked at Hunter's Inn, which would have made a total of sixteen miles, or take an expensive taxi or perhaps a bus. What, on a Sunday? 'No chance!' thought I.

However, I was told to hurry around to the main street, where the one and only bus on a Sunday was due in a few minutes. When I reached the bus stop a lady – a very large lady – was already waiting there. She was probably sixty-ish, and my unkind nature made me think, 'I hope I don't get to be that size!'

I received my comeuppance as when the bus arrived the lady beckoned me to go before her. When I said, "You were here first," her reply was "Oh, I always let the old people get on before me!"

Walking coastal paths teaches one many things!

Using my free bus pass, the bus driver took me to within two miles of my camper van, dropping me off at the end of the lane as there is no bus stop at Hunter's Inn. So all I had to do was to walk down the lane to Hunter's Inn. This was the first of several similar incidents, and I had thoroughly enjoyed my day.

At the end of the Exmoor Walking Festival we had enjoyed the coastal path so much that, mainly at Kathy's suggestion, about six of us decided to carry on walking the next thirty-five-mile section. For some of us that ended up becoming 600 miles plus! We planned to walk two weekends a year.

The second stage, Combe Martin to Barnstaple, we walked over four days the following October.

Combe Martin to Lee

For the first day's walk the group included Kathy, Jo, Mel, Gaynor, Lionel and myself. The weather was a raincoat day! The walk was graded 'strenuous in places'. We stayed at the Yarn Market Hotel in Dunster again. Antony drove us to the start of the walk at Combe Martin. The walk started with a long-drawn-out hill, which quickly sorted out the fit walkers from the unfit walkers! There were lovely views looking back to Great Hangman and Little Hangman. Later we walked through the boatyard at Watermouth and along the coast before reaching the harbour at Ilfracombe and admiring the boats moored there. We passed the house where Henry Williamson, author of *Tarka the Otter*, had lived. We had our picnic lunch on a hill overlooking Ilfracombe. The path then follows the coast through fields of sheep until it drops down into the village of Lee.

Lee to Putsborough

Weather: wet and windy
Grade: strenuous!

We had another very steep climb out of Lee, fully togged up in waterproofs. A beautiful rocky coastline, but very open and exposed to the elements. Narrow paths zigzagged their way up the cliffs with rain beating down on us. The soil is very red in that area and I remember the red water cascading down the steps like miniature waterfalls as we climbed up them. It made quite interesting photographs!

We rounded Bull Point and Morte Point, making our way to Mortehoe and Woolacombe. Here we met Antony, asking us – no, almost begging us – to call a halt to our walk because of the torrential wind and rain. I can still picture the water gushing down the sides of the roads like small rivers at Woolacombe. After asking us three times, Antony finally accepted that we wanted to continue, in spite of the rain. We were not just fair-weather walkers!

In fact by the time we reached our planned 'end of walk' at Putsborough – the further end of the two-mile beach at Morte Bay, the rain had stopped.

Antony drove us back to Dunster via Exmoor, hoping for us to see some deer. I think even the deer were sheltering from the weather! In spite of everything, we had enjoyed our day, ending with a lovely meal as always at Antony's hotel, the Yarn Market Hotel at Dunster.

A few months later, I saw Woolacombe in a different light – whilst watching my younger son, Kelvin, compete in the North Devon Marathon in boiling-hot weather!

The Path ahead

Walking in wet weather between Lee and Bull Point.

Putsborough to Braunton

Weather: good

This was a very varied walk, across rocky headlands and beaches, and beside the estuary.

From the start of our walk at Putsborough Sands, we climbed up to reach Baggy Point, which brought back memories for me, as we used to walk there as a family many years before. Lovely rocky coastline leads to Croyde Bay. Here we walked across Croyde's sandy beach and had a picnic overlooking the beach to our right and the magnificent Saunton Sands to our left.

Following a narrow path going parallel to the road, we walked to the landmark of the Saunton Sands Hotel. I somehow managed to trip and land in a heap in a shallow ditch, much to the amusement of Kathy! She asked me to stay where I was whilst she took a photograph of me! Then she helped me up! Friends – honestly!

We then entered Braunton Burrows, a very well-known area for birds and flora. The Braunton Burrows Nature Reserve has been designated a UNESCO Biosphere Reserve for its nature conservation importance. There is also a golf course and part of this area is used for military purposes.

Then we reached the twin estuary of the rivers Taw and Torridge and we followed the estuary into Braunton.

Braunton to Barnstaple

Distance: 5.5 miles

This was a short walk to finish our second section of the South West Coast Path. That day we had Keith, who sometimes led our walks, and also his wife, Jennifer. It was a very flat walk following the line of a former railway track and passing the Royal Marines airbase at Chivenor. We walked alongside the

River Taw all the way to Barnstaple to reach the historic Long Bridge. Seventy-two and a half miles had now been completed and we were still smiling and keen to do the next thirty-five miles.

Barnstaple to Appledore

Date: 25 June 2010
Distance: 15 miles
Weather: beautiful

The rest of the group had walked from Barnstaple to Westward Ho! on Mother's Day, when I was with my family – hence the reason I walked this part of the coast path on my own at a much later date.

On 25 June I left my camper van in Appledore and with my free bus pass I caught a bus to Barnstaple. It was only when I went to put my bus pass away that I realised I had, in fact, shown the bus driver my out-of-date railcard. Well, if he didn't mind, why should I? It did make me smile.

Getting off the bus, I crossed the many-arched Long Bridge to reach the point where we had finished the walk the previous year with Keith.

The first part of the walk is also part of the Tarka Trail, before reaching the former railway station at Fremington – now a tea room and museum. Carrying on along the old railway line, now resurfaced, the coastal path then turns off to reach the estuary side – later leading to the lovely sand dunes of Instow. I loved Instow! To me it resembled more of a sandy seashore, not a river estuary, with clean sand and children making sandcastles, flying kites, etc. Sunshine and blue skies – perfect!

Leaving the village of Instow behind, the coastal path continues by the side of the estuary. It seemed a long, long way and I was getting very hot and tired and I still had a long way to go. The level but tiring path eventually reached the old railway station and crossed Bideford Long Bridge.

Looking north, I could see the new Bideford Bypass bridge. Knowing that I had to pass under it, it looked a long, long way away! This was the ten-mile mark and I had five more weary miles to walk!

Towards Appledore the tide was coming in and I had to take a high-tide detour, which made the walk even longer! I had missed one of the signs, probably through tiredness, so had to retrace my steps. I eventually reached my camper van – exhausted!

It was a beautiful evening and everyone was enjoying sailing, surfing, etc., but I was too tired to even take a photograph!

Appledore to Westward Ho!

Distance: only about 5 miles

Jo had kindly offered to walk this with me. We admired the quaint narrow colourful terraced houses in Appledore, and walked across the flat salt marshes, eventually walking along the sandy beach, watching kite flyers on wheels, until we reached Westward Ho!, Where we had our lunch.

Westward Ho! to Clovelly

Date: 20 April 2009
Distance: 11.2 miles
Weather: beautiful
Leader: Keith
Grade: strenuous

About nine of us left Westward Ho! in lovely weather. John had joined us for the first time. Once we had left the holiday chalets behind, the walk was, at first, along the former track of the railway. Then the path continued along the cliff, dropping down and rising again through yellow gorse – so beautiful against the blue sea and sky. It was very hot climbing up steps, then down steps for much of the way. Further along there was a descent through woods to steps leading down to the village of Bucks Mill, where we had our lunch sitting on the shingle beach – very relaxing.

After our picnic we climbed up through bluebell woods and eventually on to a broad track known as the Hobby Drive, and again through woodland.

Whilst our group were staying in a hotel in Bideford, my daughter Paula and my two young grandchildren were using my camper van in Clovelly, and as we were walking along the Hobby Drive we met them coming to join us. The track continued over small streams, eventually ending in steps above the harbour at Clovelly. The rest of the group were met by the minibus and taken back to the hotel, whilst Paula and I and the young children hobbled up the steep cobbled street of Clovelly to Paula's car. We admired the lovely quaint cottages with troughs of flowers and hanging baskets as we made our way to the car park at the top.

A few months earlier I had injured my knee whilst walking around Hampton Court Flower Show – I didn't know walking around a flower show could be such a dangerous thing to do!

After resting it all winter, I hoped it had improved, but I had been in great pain throughout this walk and I knew that I would have to leave the group at this point. Sad! After having an operation on my knee I didn't rejoin the group until they reached Padstow, sixty-seven or so miles further down the coast.

When completing the sections I had missed with the group, I decided not to walk them necessarily in the correct order, but to do a block here and a block there, and fill in between – it seemed more achievable that way somehow. Sometimes I walked south, sometimes north, and many of the sections I walked both ways to get back to my camper van.

Clovelly to Hartland Quay

Date: 3 August 2010
Distance: 10.3 miles
Weather: fantastic

I paid £7.50 to park my camper van in the car park at Clovelly and started my walk at the top of Clovelly's lovely cobbled street. Then I passed the war memorial and walked through the woods, reaching an ornately carved roofed seat known as Angel Wings. Further on through the woodland there was a summer house built for its lovely view of the dazzling blue sea. I followed the path down through the woods to cross a narrow stream at Mouth Mill and zigzagged up a steep path through the woodland to cross several fields of sheep and cattle before zigzagging down more steps through near-shoulder-height bracken. Here I acquired a tick at the back of my neck – later removed at the local hospital.

I decided to leave the path near Windbury Point to return to my camper van at Clovelly, but instead of returning through the high bracken and woods I decided to walk back along the road. Bad move! It was six and a half miles along the busy main road on a boiling-hot day to Higher Clovelly. Then I walked down the lane to Lower Clovelly to reach my camper van.

The next day I parked at Hartland Quay – a favourite place of mine – and walked back along the coast to the point where I had left the day before. Then I turned and retraced my steps, passing the radar tower, which looks like an enormous golf ball, and the lighthouse at Hartland Point, and stopping to admire the beautiful rock strata on the quay.

Hartland Quay to Morwenstow

Date: August 2012
Distance: 7.5 miles
Grade: severe!

I camped on a farm site opposite Stoke Church – half a mile from Hartland Quay. Stoke Church is often referred to as North Devon's cathedral. The weather seemed fine, but by the time I had reached Speke's Mill and the waterfall it had started raining. I decided to continue, hoping the weather would improve. It did – as I walked through the valley – and the rest of the day was beautiful.

There's one thing I had forgotten about walking in August! I was wearing a pair of shorts and had forgotten about overgrown brambles stretching across some of the paths and steps, but even worse were the biting horseflies! My legs looked like a battlefield. No more shorts for me that year!

I reached Welcombe Mouth and after a rest I climbed back up the steep hill and returned the same way to my camper van. There were great views in both directions.

The next morning I parked at Morwenstow Tea Rooms, beside the church, and walked to the coastal path, then northwards. This walk was classed as 'severe' – and it was! For my sins it would mean I had to walk there and back to my camper van. "Do I do this for fun?" I asked myself. The river valleys (I think there were four) were deep and steep, and of course I crossed the same four going back to my camper van. This section is definitely not for the faint-hearted!

Marsland Mouth marks the Cornish/North Devon border, with the unusual county sign. I believe this is the only county sign on the whole path. It is made of wood with the county badge on the right-hand side and the words 'Cornwall' and (underneath) 'Kernow' (Cornish for Cornwall). This is immediately followed by the next steep ascent to the top of Marsland Cliff. Then there is a steep descent with lots of steps to a footbridge, then a steep climb up the hill. Later there is a grassy descent to a small footbridge overlooking Yeol Mouth. Then there is another steep climb to the top of Henna Cliff, followed by a steep descent to cross a footbridge. Steps then lead on to Vicarage Cliff and down again to the footpath into the village of Morwenstow to reach my camper van. I ended the day with a meal at the tea rooms, putting back on all the calories I had walked off!

It only occurred to me later that having walked every inch of the coastal path going north to Welcombe Mouth (where I had left off the previous day) I could have avoided the steep ascents and descents – particularly the steep descent down Henna Cliff – on my return, by going across the fields to my camper van. Oh no! A glutton for punishment, I did the coast path on my own both ways!

A few days later, without walking in between, my left knee became swollen with fluid and was painful. Would I never learn?

According to the South West Coast Path Association, when walking the 630-mile path one goes up or down 30,000 steps – I can well believe it!

Morwenstow to Bude

Date: 28 June 2010
Distance: 7.9 miles

Fortunately for me, my campsite at Bude adjoined the coastal path. I walked northwards, intending to walk for three hours before turning back, but unfortunately that left me in no-man's-land, so I decided to carry on, hoping some form of transport would be available to get me back to Bude – perhaps an expensive taxi!

I walked by Crooklets Beach, Maer Cliff, Sandymouth and Duckpool, and the satellite dishes, which were only specks on the horizon when I left Bude, were now towering above me. I continued by Hawker's Hut, which is now owned by the National Trust. The hut was built of driftwood by the Reverend Hawker on what is known as Vicarage Cliff, and here it is said he wrote his sermons and books. He was the Vicar of Morwenstow and the church is the nearest building to the cliff.

Morwenstow is a very isolated village, and I was getting concerned about how I was going to get back to my camper van without having to walk back along the 7.9 miles of coastal path.

I went into the tea rooms opposite Morwenstow Church and asked rather tongue-in-cheek, "I don't suppose you know anything about buses around here?"

Back came the reply, looking at the clock, "There is only one bus today and that goes in seven minutes. If you hurry, you will be able to catch it."

So I had to go without my cream tea in the tea rooms! But I was very grateful for a free bus back to Bude, from where I walked on the coast path back to my campsite. Someone was looking after me!

Several days later I drove back to Morwenstow Tea Rooms, on a very wet day, and enjoyed a lovely lunch whilst having a very interesting conversation with another walker – a young man who was 'wild camping' whilst walking the coast path. There is a great camaraderie between walkers – whatever their age or gender!

Bude to Widemouth Bay

Date: June 2010

Staying at the campsite just north of Bude, I decided to walk to Widemouth Bay and back one evening. At first the coast path follows alongside the Bude Canal, which has houses and cottages on one side with lovely displays of flowers in hanging baskets. The path climbs up on to a cliff ridge by the Compass Point Tower – an octagonal tower said to match the Tower of the Winds at Athens.

The coast path is easy walking on the downland over Efford Beacon, from where extensive views could be seen both north and south. The path later drops down into Widemouth Bay, where there is a good stretch of sandy beach and a holiday village.

Widemouth Bay to Crackington Haven

Date: August 2013
Distance: 7miles
Graded: strenuous

I camped for two nights at Penhalt Farm Campsite, with its lovely views of the dramatic coastline northward of Bude.

Leaving my camper van at Widemouth Bay Car Park, I set out intending to walk halfway to Crackington Haven and then return to my camper van. As I was leaving Widemouth I saw on the cliffs a group of young people being taught rock climbing. The path climbed steeply up for a short distance on to the road until it reached a car park on the top of Penhalt Cliff, which had lovely views.

At the far end of the car park, the path went back on to the cliff edge, from where there is a steep descent on to the small beach of Millock Haven. It was worthwhile to walk a short way along the pebble beach to look at the remarkable rock strata. North Devon and Cornwall have some very dramatic folded strata, but here at Millock Haven the strata is in a chevron pattern.

It was also good to take a breather before the long steep trek up the narrow road, before turning right on to the cliff path at Raven's Beak. The heathland here was covered in heather in full bloom – beautiful against the deep blue sea and cloudless blue sky.

The path continued to climb steadily, passing along field edges before dropping down through an ancient woodland known as the Dizzard, with wooden planks over small streams. I decided at this point to push on to Crackington Haven and, hopefully, catch a bus back to Widemouth Bay and my camper van.

The climbs up were steep – little did I know they would get steeper! And the descents would get even steeper and deeper! Some of the climbs down were so steep that I couldn't see the bottom of the valley I was walking into! In fact one path looked as if it ended straight in the sea! Nor in places could I see the top of the hill when climbing up. In one place I remember seeing horses grazing above me, but they looked as small as dogs. In another place the uphill steps were so steep I went on my hands and knees, thinking, 'I can't go on any more.' Then I had cramp in both calf muscles. Painful or what! And I was doing this for fun! I eventually got to the top.

Not long afterwards I passed a couple sitting down having a drink and a rest. They asked me what I thought of the last steep hill. I said my book had described it well: 'It will test your heart and lungs!' It did! They also asked where I was walking from and to. I said I had left my camper van at Widemouth Bay and hoped I would be able to catch a bus at Crackington Haven.

As it happened, the walk had taken so much longer than planned, due to the severity of it, that I would have missed the bus anyway.

Eventually the couple overtook me when I had stopped for a drink and a rest. When I had reached the top of yet another hill – the last before dropping down into Crackington Haven – I found the same couple waiting for me, to ask if I would like a lift back to Widemouth Bay. They had left one of their cars in the same car park as my camper van, and their second car nearby St Gennys Church. They kindly gave me a lift back.

I have found such kindness from walkers all along the coast path.

The next day all I had to do was make use of the free parking at St Gennys Church and walk down the steep hill around the coast path and into Crackington Haven, where I enjoyed lunch at a beachside café before climbing back up the steep hill and returning to my camper van. Then I drove back to the campsite at Widemouth Bay.

Crackington Haven to Boscastle

Date: June
Distance: 6.7 miles
Weather: beautiful
Grade: severe

Usually when doing a long section I would start at one end, walk to the middle and then walk back to my camper van. But on this walk, Crackington Haven to Boscastle (and from Boscastle to Tintagel) I parked in the middle, near Highcliff, and the first day I walked to Crackington Haven and on the second day I walked south to Boscastle.

I parked my camper van on a minor road behind Highcliff, and I'll always remember the lane for the hedges were draped with honeysuckle, and the high banks were ablaze with red/purple foxgloves against a cloudless blue sky.

I walked through to the coast path, turned right and followed the path. I didn't find it as difficult as I had expected. No doubt the difficult section is between Boscastle and Tintagel!

Reaching Crackington Haven, I bought an ice cream and stayed for a little while watching families on the beach before turning back and following the coast path back to my camper van.

The next day I parked again in the same minor road. I rejoined the coast path, but turned left towards Boscastle past Highcliff – the highest cliff in Cornwall. It was steep in places, particularly on the downhill section.

The path then went down through an isolated valley among gorse bushes and banks of thrift, over a footbridge and up the steep slopes of Rusey Cliff. Then I walked through pastures for several fields of cows and calves and then down cliffside steps to Fire Beacon Point; I walked up more steps over Beeny Cliff and down some steps, and back up 189 more steps before reaching a level area with stone walls showing white quartz boulders, before coming to Pentargon and the mast at Penally Point.

I admired the lovely views back along the coast before taking the path down into lovely Boscastle for lunch at the Harbour Light Café.

The original building was a converted chapel, but it had been completely swept away in the flash floods of 2004. Since then it has been rebuilt exactly as it was before the flood.

I met some lovely walkers, including a couple from Oregon, USA.

I walked back to my camper van along the lanes.

Boscastle to Tintagel

Date: June 2011
Distance: 4.6 miles

This is one of my favourite stretches of the coast path. I walked it on my own, enjoying the beautiful scenery. Passing the White Customs Tower, there were views of the coastline stretching away both north and south.

Leaving Boscastle, I had to walk over the bridge – now rebuilt after the floods – and alongside the narrow inlet that leads to the mouth of the river. At the entrance of the harbour I was thrilled to watch my first blowhole as the waves crashed against the cliffs.

The path has several uphill and downhill sections. I remember the section for the rock arch known as the Ladies Window, and as I was taking a photograph a man chose that moment to stand in the Ladies Window!

The path then descended into an exquisite rocky valley where there was a footbridge and stream with the surging waves beyond. From the footbridge, the path climbs again around the edge of the grassy area of Bossiney Common and above the sandy bay of Bossiney Haven. The path continues to Barras Nose headland and drops down to Tintagel and the Castle Hotel on the headland.

The Ladies Window, between Boscastle and Tintagel.
(I'm not quite sure what a man is doing in a ladies' window!)

Tintagel to Trebarwith Strand

Distance: 3.5 miles
Grade: easy

I left my camper van on the Headland Campsite near to the Castle Hotel in Tintagel and joined the path at the Barras Nose headland and walked around the headland to the castle ruins.

Taking the steps by the side of the ruins, the path overlooked The Island – lovely views!

To the left, in isolation, stands Tintagel Church, dedicated to St Materiana, and ahead on the cliff is the youth hostel – in a superb location!

The path was easy going, but the coastline became very rugged.

In earlier centuries this section of the coast was heavily quarried for slate, with up to 1,000 men being employed in the trade. Delabole Village (Delabole meaning slate in Cornish) is just inland.

Especially photogenic was the tall pillar of rock with the offshore Gull Rock in the background. Here too was a beautiful herringbone slate wall, which I took a photograph of – a work of art!

The path dropped down to the bay at Trebarwith Strand, which was crowded on such a lovely day.

I love the Cornish stone and slate walls – such works of art.

Trebarwith Strand to Port Isaac

Date: 3 April
Distance: 6 miles
Grade: severe

Elizabeth, who is a walking friend from home, offered to walk this section with me. We had stayed the night before at a National Trust farm – Tresmorn Farm at Crackington Haven.

After parking in a large car park above the harbour at Trebarwith Strand, we walked past the Portwilliam Pub and climbed the 202 steps up the rock face behind and above the pub.

There were some level stretches of grass fields and then there were more steep-sided paths, some of which were bordered with blackthorn hedges covered in white blossom. There were also gorse bushes that were covered in bright-yellow blooms, scenting the air with their coconut-like perfume.

We saw a number of cock pheasants and a large number of skylarks, both flying and settling on the gorse bushes. There were primroses and violets, particularly on the sides of the streams that meandered down the steep-sided valleys, one valley opening out to end in a waterfall.

We saw walls topped with white quartz and seams of quartz in the rock strata.

Gull Rock, the island just offshore at Trebarwith Strand, stayed in sight the whole length of the walk.

The path continued in and out of deep valleys, the deepest being at Jacket's Point.

We also saw the opening of the tunnel called Donkey Hole at Barrett's Zawn, which was followed by yet another steep valley.

Eventually the path led to a road as we neared Port Gaverne, where a cluster of houses was being built on the clifftop. These houses will have spectacular sea views!

The small beach, now quiet, used to be busy with slate being loaded on to ships.

The path departs from Port Gaverne by the roadside pavement, rising steeply to enter Port Isaac by the car park and the Bay Hotel.

A narrow path follows the coast around to join the main steep street of Port Isaac, with tourist shops on either side and the harbour entrance at the bottom of the hill. There are narrow alleys leading off. Quaint cottages, cafés, pubs and the lifeboat station can also be found.

We took a taxi back to my camper van.

Port Isaac to the Padstow Ferry

Date: July

I parked my camper van at the top of Port Isaac and walked down through the picturesque village of Port Isaac with its narrow lanes and harbour, not forgetting that it provided the setting for the TV programme *Doc Martin*!

Reaching the harbour, I decided to take the alternative path to Port Quin, across the fields, and return along the coast path, making it a circular route.

On the way I met a lovely Canadian couple who, whilst I was talking to them, insisted on giving me a new memory stick as my camera suddenly flashed up 'Memory Stick Full' – such kindness! They were just finishing their first walking holiday in Britain and had found walkers so friendly. It was their way of saying thank you.

Reaching Port Quin, I returned to Port Isaac by taking the coast path and was able, with my new memory stick, to take photographs of the rocky coastline and the harbour as I returned to Port Isaac.

I had tea in the Old School Room, which was featured in the TV programme *Doc Martin*.

When I returned to my camper van, I had a note tucked into the windscreen asking if I was interested in selling my camper van – not for the first time!

That night I camped at a campsite adjoining the farm shop and restaurant – I'm not daft!

The next day I parked at the National Trust car park near Rumps Point and joined the coast path to walk north to Port Quin.

I had planned to buy a cup of coffee, an ice cream or a cream tea, but found only a few cottages. I read up afterwards that it had once been a thriving fishing port. I therefore had to retrace my steps back to my camper van and make my own cuppa (life can be hard at times!).

After moving my camper van to a car park at Daymer Bay, I first walked along the beach – as the tide was out – to the Padstow ferry at Rock, returning via the sand dunes (the coastal path).

I visited St Enodoc Church, which was hidden behind a thick hedge, grown to protect the church from windblown sand. The church had been nearly buried by sand from the nearby beaches on several occasions. Sir John Betjeman is buried in the churchyard. As I was leaving the churchyard I was amazed to see a war grave of a crewman from HMS *Charybdis* – Eric Booth's ship – which had been torpedoed between France and the Channel Islands during World War Two. Most of the bodies were washed ashore in the Channel Islands and were buried in the Howard Davis Park in St Helier, Jersey, which my friend Jean (Eric's wife) and I had visited the previous year.

Leaving the churchyard, I walked north to Polzeath – a great surfing beach and very crowded on such a lovely day. And then on I went to Rumps Point, where I had walked the previous day. I then retraced my steps to Daymer Bay and my camper van.

NB: The ferry from Rock operates all year, crossing the river to Padstow.

I had now caught up with my walking friends!

Padstow to Treyarnon

Date: 15 October 2010
Distance: 11.6 miles

Three cheers. I was back walking with the group! The group consisted of Kathy, Jo, Mel, myself, Gaynor and Lionel, Debbie and John. We stayed at the Whipsiderry Hotel at Porth, just north of Newquay, which is a lovely family hotel. We enjoyed a six-course evening meal ready for the next day's walk.

Leaving two cars at Treyarnon Beach, we took the other two cars to Padstow to start our walk. Our first stop was the pasty and sandwich shop in Padstow before walking out to the headland past the harbour. The first part of the walk followed the Camel Estuary before going around the exposed headland of Stepper Point with its lookout tower.

Some of the coast was very rocky; other parts had beautiful sandy beaches, such as near Trevone and particularly Harlyn Bay.

We walked past Rick Stein's house at Mother Ivey's Bay and by the lifeboat station. Also nearby we were delighted to see a seal bobbing up and down in the water.

We walked to Trevose Head and later the beautiful beaches of Booby's Bay and Constantine Bay.

Our walk ended at the sandy beach at Treyarnon to reach our cars.

Treyarnon to Porth

Date: 16 October 2010
Distance:11.1 miles

The next day was a beautiful day, more like summer than October! Our walk started where we had left off the day before at Treyarnon. More lovely sandy beaches and rocky headlands with often a few rocky islands just off the shore.

Today's walk took us by one of Cornwall's fabulous beaches at

31

Bedruthan Steps with its many outcrops of pinnacles/islands. The tide was in.

By the time we had had our lunch at the National Trust café at Bedruthan Steps and reached Watergate Bay, the tide was going out and it was decided to walk along the beach – boots off – paddling through the edge of the tide. Things didn't quite go according to plan as the tide wasn't going out quickly enough for us to skirt around the isolated rocks. There was nothing for it but for us to scramble over the rocks barefooted. The rocks were covered in barnacles until we were clear of the tide! Occasionally a rogue wave came in and someone (but not me!) got their knickers wet – all part of the fun!

From the beach we had to climb 135 steep steps, finding ourselves nearly opposite the short road to our hotel to reach the end of our 11.1-mile walk. An excellent day.

Another fabulous six-course meal completed the day.

Porth to Holywell

Date: Sunday 17 October

We left the cars at the hotel and walked from the hotel across Porth Sands into Newquay, where some of us bought Cornish pasties for our lunches. We walked by Newquay Fish Market to join the coastal path.

Leaving Newquay Harbour behind, we climbed past the Old Huer's Hut (from where we get the expression hue and cry – shouting when the shoals of fish were seen coming in). We noted a lot of new buildings and hotels being built on the clifftop. We crossed the famous Fistral Beach, known for surfing, where there was a surfing contest taking place.

Later the lovely Crantock Beach came into view, but first we had to negotiate the Gannel Estuary by walking upstream to cross over a small wooden bridge. Had we been a bit later, with the tide coming in so fast, we would have had to go even further upstream to cross. Coastal walking isn't always straightforward!

After having our picnic lunch we continued our walk until we reached Holywell Beach, where we celebrated the end of this year's walking by taking off our boots to paddle in the sea, which for October was quite unbelievably warm. We ended at the pub for coffee whilst we waited for our taxi back to our hotel at Porth.

Approximately 200 miles completed! Only another 430 miles to go!

Holywell to Porthtowan

Date: 3 April
Distance: 12.5 miles
Weather: sunny

We stayed at a hotel in Portreath and started our walk at the Piran's Inn at Holywell, where we had left off walking five months earlier. The weather was the same as it had been the previous October – brilliant sunshine and blue sky – and the sea was so blue it looked unreal.

Rocky coastline until we reached the two-mile stretch of Perranporth Sands, backed by steep sand dunes. With the tide out we were able to walk along the beautiful beach, at the end of which we had our picnic lunch.

The afternoon walk took us past the youth hostel and along the cliffs. Mining evidence was shown by the now disused chimneys and warning notices of mineshafts, some of which were now covered by iron grills to allow bats to enter. There were exposed rocks containing iron and arsenic.

We passed St Agnes Head and, Towanroath's iconic engine house. There are disused tin and copper mines on this section.

We stopped for a 'hedgehog' ice cream at Chapel Forth, before climbing yet another hill into Porthtowan.

It had been a varied walk with rocky coastline, sandy beaches, old mining areas, spectacular scenery, primroses, violets and golden gorse.

A reminder of Cornwall's past. The now deserted Wheal Coates mine. During its lifetime the mine produced 717 tons of tin and 335 tons of copper.

Porthtowan to Godrevy

Date: 4 April
Distance: 11.5 miles
Weather: glorious sunshine

This walk will be especially remembered for the weather as well as the scenery. Quite a lot of high headland walking, but also some steep steps up and down several valleys (just to step over a stream about eighteen inches wide!). Some of the walk followed a Ministry of Defence fence, which seemed to go on for mile after mile!

We reached Portreath, where our hotel was, but we carried on along the headland – again violets and carpets of primroses everywhere. Our biggest thrill that day was peering over into a bay between Navax Point and Godrevy Point – the steep sides of the cliffs were covered in primroses and on the rocks at least nine seals were counted basking in the sunshine, with several more bobbing up and down in the deep-blue sea. A moment to remember for ever.

We ended the day in the National Trust café at Godrevy eating coffee-and-walnut cake whilst waiting for our taxi back to the hotel.

Godrevy to St Ives

Date: 5 April
Distance: 10 miles
Weather: gale-force winds and rain

The walkers were Kathy, Jo, Mel, John, Lionel and Gaynor, Keith and myself. We struggled the ten miles into the teeth of a gale along the three miles of Hayle Beach, and then along the boring roadside, walking past Lelant Station. We walked by the golf course on the other side of the estuary, where we had our picnic in the pouring rain overlooking a rather soggy beach.

The path continued on the seaward side of a single-track narrow railway, followed by a very narrow slippery woodland path with primroses on both sides.

Later there were views of the three-mile stretch of sand behind us and Carbis Bay ahead. We passed another Huer's Hut. The path continued to follow the coast to reach the outskirts of St Ives.

With the weather brightening we wandered around St Ives and bought an ice cream. Here there were notices that said 'DO NOT FEED THE SEAGULLS'! Chance would be a fine thing! One cheeky seagull swooped down and grabbed my ice cream out of my hand before I had had the chance to take one lick!

We saw a flock of turnstones on the beach among the pebbles – so aptly named, as we watched them turning pebbles over!

We returned to our hotel by taxi.

St Ives to Zennor Head

Date: 6 April
Distance: 7 miles

The Coast Path Walk Book gives two warnings at the start of this St Ives to Zennor Head walk:

1. It is the start of the most deserted stretch of coast on the whole South West Coast Path.

2. The path is rough and rocky, the terrain is severe and yet, after rain it can be surprisingly boggy – a few will average two miles (3 km) an hour.

In other words it may take walkers a lot longer than they expect. It did!

We parked our cars at the St Ives Leisure Centre and the first part of the walk took us through St Ives town and by the Tate, having walked the island section the previous day.

Although the coastal scenery was beautiful, more attention had to be given to the boulder-strewn path – it was certainly slow going!

The coast path leads out to the rugged Clodgy Point, then Hor Point and Pen Enys Point, and later reaches a trig point on Carn Naun with extensive views both back and onwards towards Zennor Head and the lighthouse at Pendeen Watch.

At Zennor Head we walked inland to where our spare cars were parked at the Old Methodist Chapel (now converted into a backpackers' hostel). We then transferred our luggage to the Old Success Inn at Sennen Cove.

Zennor Head to Sennen Cove

Date: 7 April

I remember this as a hard, hard day! We were dropped off at the backpackers' hostel and walked seaward to rejoin the coast path. We continued from Zennor Head to Gurnard's Head and Bosigran, an Iron Age fort.

The path was confusing in places and went inland through gorse bushes, aiming for the highest point and passing through a gap in a low wall before turning right and continuing up to the top of the ridge, only then to descend to cross a small bridge over a stream by a ruined building. We followed the path around the back of Portheras Cove and on to the lighthouse at Pendeen Watch.

The coast between Pendeen Watch and Botallack brings into focus all of Cornwall's missing past – Geevan Tin Mine, Levant Beam Engine House and other relics of the past are in this area.

By taking a narrower path seaward of the wide gravel track, we were able to get a better view of the cliffside.

Botallack Engine Houses are now of course in ruins.

Ahead of us could be seen the unmistakable shape of Cape Cornwall and its chimney-like tower. Just before we reached there, the path took us through narrow lanes and across a pasture where two donkeys enjoyed our pats of admiration.

As we climbed to the chimney on the top of Cape Cornwall we could hardly stand against the strong winds, and soon we continued on our way to our Sennen Cove hotel by taxi.

The next day we returned to Cape Cornwall, and after crossing a small field we continued on the coast path – not littered by boulders as on previous days, but a huge rock had to be negotiated, with much laughter.

Eventually we dropped down to a lovely sandy beach at Whitesand Bay, which curved all the way to Sennen Cove. With the tide out – guess what? Walking boots off, we walked through the low lapping waves to our hotel at the end of the beach – the

Old Success Inn at Sennen Cove. We enjoyed a leisurely afternoon as it had been only a five-mile walk.

I have since been back to this beach (Whitesand Bay) at Sennen on a perfect summer's day and it looked like a beach in the Caribbean! Cloudless blue sky and deep-blue sea further out with turquoise waves all around the bay.

Sennen Cove to Penberth Cove

Date: April
Distance: 9 miles
Weather: beautiful

This walk will be remembered as one of the loveliest sections, far easier than the previous two days! And we saw red-legged choughs.

Our walk started from our hotel, along the seafront and past the Round House, which is now used as an art gallery. We climbed steps to join the headland coast path. A little further on we were able to see the offshore islands and the Longships Lighthouse in the distance.

The path goes around the Land's End Hotel and a shopping complex – it's sad in a way to see how Land's End is now so commercialised. When I first visited Land's End, in the late 1950s, it was just one building surrounded by open downland.

We had photographs taken at the iconic white Land's End fingerpost.

This is a beautiful section of the coast path, especially where the path hugs the rocky coast. The sea was a beautiful turquoise and the cliffs have several arches, one named the Armed Knight.

The path went down some rocky steps then climbed to the coastguard station on Gwennap Head.

At Porthgwarra we walked down the slipway on to the beach and walked through the Fisherman's Tunnel to rejoin the coastal path and continue to Porth Chapel.

We had our picnic lunch overlooking a peaceful beach and

then continued on our walk until we reached the Minack open-air theatre – what an ideal position overlooking the sea!

Here the coast path drops steeply at the cliff edge, where a notice warns: 'A difficult descent – not recommended for young children or elderly persons'.

Ha! Who of us is elderly? Well, I'm young at heart – other parts older! We negotiated it safely.

The views across to Porthcurno Beach were as good as any Mediterranean beach view and the water was deep turquoise. I will always be able to picture that beach with the Logan Rock at the far end.

We continued our walk to Penberth Cove, then walked up through the village to await our taxi.

Two hundred and sixty-three miles completed; 367 left to do!

Here the coastal path drops steeply to Porthcurno Beach below. The notice at the top said, 'A difficult descent – not recommended for children or the elderly'! Look how small the people on the beach look.

Penberth Cove to Marazion

Date: 21 October
Grade: strenuous, then easier

The walkers were Gaynor and Lionel, Mel, John, myself and Keith, and Jo joined us the next day. Sadly Kathy was not able to be with us.

We were staying at the Marazion Hotel at Marazion, just over the road from the slipway to St Michael's Mount. Keith's wife, Jennifer, had also joined us at the hotel, but was not walking.

At Penberth Cove we crossed the slipway and started the steep climb out of the cove. The path continued along the clifftop with lovely sea views. Having just come up, it didn't seem long before we had a steep descent and then a climb at Porthguarnon.

The path had been very boulder-strewn and it was slow going. Then the path went a little inland and a white painted sign on a granite boulder (where are the signposts when you need them?) directed us to turn right.

The path nearing St Loy eventually descended steeply through woodland and passed a few cottages. Then it continued on to a very boulder-strewn beach – very large boulders. The coast path was again visible.

The path climbed to pass above the lighthouse at Tater-Du. We then crossed another boulder-strewn landscape with the path dropping steeply down into Lamorna Cove, which we walked along and up the other side.

The path – well marked – eventually led to a tarmac road, which descended into Mousehole. The road leads to the harbour and past picturesque cottages. The route became very urban and we could easily have lost the official path through car parks, down lanes, through Newlyn's famous fish markets and on to Penzance.

The path follows the sea wall around St Michael's Bay with St Michael's Mount getting ever nearer until we reached our hotel in Marazion.

After arriving at the hotel, several of us walked over the causeway to St Michael's Mount, as the tide was conveniently out.

Marazion to Porthleven

Date: 22 October
Distance: 10.6 miles

Leaving the hotel, we had to go along the road as there seemed no recognisable path along the beach. Just as we reached the outskirts of Marazion, and the speed-restriction sign, we were able to turn right into a driveway before going down some concrete steps to follow the path to the shoreline.

The view of St Michael's Mount is superb from this angle and the island remains a focal point throughout the sweep of Mount's Bay. We crossed the top of the beach to some metal steps.

Just after Trenow Cove the path reaches a track and goes inland and then right to follow low cliffs to Perranuthnoe.

Taking a lane on the seaward side of the car park, we had to go right and then left into a field. Then there was a well-marked path to Cudden Point, from where there were lovely views before we descended to Praa Sands. We passed a restored engine house and walked to Trewavas Head and then on to Porthleven.

Porthleven to Kynance Cove

Date: 23 October
Weather: gale-force winds and torrential rain!
Leader: Keith

I think that day will always be remembered for its weather and the sad fact that it would be the last time most of us would see Keith before he died of cancer, less than two months later. None of us were aware that he was ill. Keith was a lovely man and a very enthusiastic walker, and our sympathies go out to Jennifer.

Porthleven lies three miles south-west of Helston, midway round the arc of Mount's Bay. The path sets off by the coastguard lookout above Porthleven Sands. Ahead lay Lee Bar and, immediately to our left, Loe Pool (once a tidal inlet, but now blocked in by the

41

shingle strip). This area has known tragedy, both in the lake and on the shore, where 120 lives were lost in a shipwreck.

The whole Cornish coast – particularly the North Cornish coast – has been a graveyard for many ships blown on to the rugged coastline.

We could only imagine the force of the winter storms as we (in October) were walking against a gale-force headwind. In places it brought us to a standstill as we tried to walk forward, and once as Keith was climbing over a stile with a loaded rucksack he nearly got blown over.

The path continues ascending and descending to Gunwalloe fishing cove. Then there is a stiff pull up to 200 feet above Halzephron Cove.

After following a broad track uphill past Mullion Golf Course, we dropped down again to Poldhu Cove – very popular in summer for its sandy beach. From sea level we walked up a steep private drive to what is now a residential home, formerly a clifftop hotel, before reaching steps above the beach.

After a short walk round Poldhu Point we reached the Marconi Monument, where the first transatlantic signals were transmitted in December 1901. From this spot Morse code was transmitted 3,000 miles to St John's, Newfoundland.

With spectacular coastal views, the path dipped through Polurrian, climbed in front of cliff cottages to a road by Mullion Cove Hotel, and then led down steps seaward into Mullion Cove, with Mullion Island just offshore.

After Mullion Cove, the land plateaus out with views of exposed and very windswept bays and coves. From 300 feet above sea level we were fortunate enough to see several red-legged choughs now hopefully recolonising the Cornish coast on this Lizard National Nature Reserve. We saw a number of Shetland ponies grazing – no doubt their shaggy coats helped keep out the wind and now torrential rain.

When we reached Kynance Cove we stopped for coffee and cake at the small café – partly to shelter from the wild weather.

At that point Keith decided it would be safer to stop the walk because of the weather conditions and the danger of being blown off the coastal path. We waited for the waves to recede in the tiny bay before dashing across the short stretch of beach and making our way to the car park to order our taxi.

Kynance Cove to the Lizard

Date: 24 October
Weather: wet, wet, wet!

The walkers were Gaynor and Lionel, John, Mel, Jo and myself. Keith and Jennifer had returned home for a hospital appointment.

This was a short walk to finish the walk we had to abandon the day before.

The Lizard is the most southerly point of England – the only place in the UK which lies below the 50-degrees parallel.

We took a group photograph at the end of the walk above the lifeboat station before heading to the café. I remember we had to stand to drink our coffee as the rain poured off our wet-weather gear! We finished our day by buying 'real' Cornish pasties to take home.

I had planned to camp on the way home, but the weather was so bad I decided to drive straight home, stopping for rest stops en route. I arrived home tired, but happy with what we had accomplished.

The Lizard to Coverack

Date: 27 April
Distance: 10.4 miles
Weather: in spite of rain being forecast, dry all day, getting brighter, with sunshine and blue sky.
Grade: moderate, strenuous in places

We were staying at a hotel in Helston. There were seven of us in the group: Kathy, Mel, Jo, Gaynor and Lionel, Debbie and

43

myself. Our taxi left at 9.30 a.m. to take us to the Lizard so we could join the coast path where we left off the previous autumn – above the old coastguard station and the small café, which is the most southerly café in Great Britain.

This section of cliffs and coves is largely sheltered from the worst of the prevailing south-westerly winds and consequently has a lush pasture-type character. This area is also less visited and substantial stretches are quiet and remote.

The coast path passes in front of the lighthouse and the youth hostel. Thrift was in bloom on the path sides. We saw a herd of Shetland ponies near the Lloyds Signal Station.

An isolated house had a steep garden full of camellias in bloom, as well as early azaleas flowering beside a running stream. We also saw bluebells and primroses.

A dramatic viewpoint looked down on the Devil's Frying Pan – owned by the National Trust (the area not the frying pan!).

The path eventually dropped down into the little picturesque harbour of Cadgwith, with thatched cottages edging the narrow lane, some with chains over the roof.

We saw honeysuckle in full bloom (in April!) as well as other spring flowers.

We had our coffee and snack sitting on a bench opposite the harbour entrance, where they were clearing seaweed, probably left by the winter storms – no doubt to deposit on someone's garden to produce some gorgeous early potatoes.

The path climbs up the other side of the harbour with views back over the harbour and along the coast we had walked earlier in the day. Later the path descended to Poltesco, crossing a footbridge. The path forks here, but both ways reach the same point. Climbing out of Poltesco, the path then joins a road which leads to the beach at Kennack Sands, which we walked across before stopping for our picnic lunch – a lovely spot. By then the sun had come out and the sea and sky were a lovely blue.

We climbed over a variety of stiles – stone stiles and ladder stiles.

The path goes right in front of a house and on to the cliffs to reach the headland of Carrick Luz, an Iron Age fort. We walked down into a rocky valley and over a footbridge, and eventually along lanes to drop down into Coverack with its little harbour. There we enjoyed a delicious ice cream before walking around the bay to meet our taxi. On the way back to our hotel it poured with rain!

Coverack to Helford

Date: 28 April 2012
Distance: 13 miles
Weather: cloudy

This walk will be remembered for its mud, mud, mud! And also it was to be my last day's walking with the group. We were reaching the halfway marker (315 miles) from the start of our walk at Minehead.

A long hard day! The thirteen miles included walking around the creek – instead of removing our boots and socks to wade across.

Our walk started by passing cottages with colourful gardens. Then came a very low-lying/sea-level area known as Lowland Point, and eventually we walked through the now closed quarry. Regretfully we saw no seals, which can sometimes be seen in this area. The path then diverted inland through muddy fields – well, more correctly described as liquid manure (especially by a cattle feeding trough) that we had to plough through – before reaching a stile!

A narrow lane took us through Rosenithon, a small hamlet of a few cottages, one having a genuine Gypsy caravan in its lovely garden.

We skirted ploughed fields, walked along narrow lanes, across pastures and through mud before climbing over more stiles. The path led down to a road, eventually leading to the tiny hamlet of Porthoustock. The path then went inland to avoid a quarry. Later we walked along an enclosed path, which led to a track between buildings. From there a tarmac road led down into Porthallow – the official halfway point of the 630-mile South West Coast Path.

Standing in front of the official stone marker, we cracked open a bottle of champagne, kindly donated by Kathy, who also provided the glasses. No one can ever imagine what walkers carry in their rucksacks! I once carried an iced cake and a carving knife, for a surprise cake-cutting, to celebrate our club's twenty-first birthday! Ramblers are anything but dull and boring!

Only another 315 miles to the end of the walk.

Leaving the beach by steep steps, we arrived at the headland, which has lovely views towards the Helford river, Falmouth and Pendennis Castle. We had our lunch sitting on a beach overlooking the estuary. We decided not to wade through the creek, but climbed quite steeply up and along lanes that took us around the creek – including a lane with steep banks of bluebells. Then we walked through bluebell woods with very muddy paths and also wild garlic, eventually ending in the car park at Helford by the tea rooms, where we enjoyed a well-earned cup of tea and cake whilst we waited for our taxi.

That evening we enjoyed what I thought would be my final meal with the group, opening another bottle of champagne to wish them well. I am delighted to say they continued and completed their walk in October 2015. I joined them to walk their final section and help them celebrate with – you've guessed it – champagne. There was also a beautiful cake, provided by Gaynor and Lionel, depicting a map of Devon, Cornwall, Dorset, etc. Around the base was a little figure of each of us, complete with rucksacks, boots, etc., and the words 'WE DID IT!'

From Helford I intended carrying on at my own pace – never in a million years thinking I would ever complete it.

Yes, walking the coast path really does become addictive! But I tell myself there are worse addictions.

Halfway marker at Porthallow – only another 315 miles to walk!

Helford to the St Mawes Ferry

Date: 4 May 2017
Distance: 10.3 miles
Grade: moderate

It was at this point that I left the group in April 2012, having meanwhile walked the coast of Dorset and other sections on my own.

I had reverted to my previous plan of not necessarily walking the path in the correct order, but I have since written them in the correct order to make more sense when reading through it. Also, during my last year of walking the path I had a friend who, although not walking with me, dropped me off at the start of my walks and picked me up at the end of the day – which was a great help to me.

I found this walk from Helford Estuary one of the best walks on this whole section of coast, especially as I was walking in springtime with all the bluebells in flower.

I was dropped off at the top of the lane leading down to the ferry point and the Ferryboat Inn. I found the acorn sign of the coastal path and turned left up steps to a grassy hill, following the track until it dropped down past a private beach belonging to the Trebah Gardens at Polgwidden Cove. From this very beach in 1944 American troops made their way over to Omaha Beach in Normandy for the D-Day landings.

The path reached the small hamlet at Durgen and later I stopped to admire the view at the end of the estuary.

As I was going through the kissing gate I saw a young adder slithering away in the grass, and I was able to photograph it.

It was a fantastic walk around and into Maenporth Beach – a great surfing beach.

The path climbed up behind the beach café and continued to Swanpool Beach through a lovely bluebell wood.

Later Gyllyngvase Beach was the beginning of urban Falmouth. From there I followed acorn signs along the one-way road around Pendennis Point and Castle.

The path emerges from woods, and following signs, I eventually entered Falmouth's main shopping street and arrived at the Prince of Wales Pier and the ferry point to St Mawes.

The first of the two adders I saw.

48

St Mawes to Portscatho

Date: May 2017
Distance: 6.2 miles
Grade: easy

Two ferries are required: the first to cross from Falmouth to St Mawes and the second ferry to cross from St Mawes to Place.

I started the day by catching the ferry taxi to Place. Leaving the jetty and reaching the other side, the path went in front of Place House, an enormous country mansion, and shortly afterwards I reached the lovely St Anthony in Roseland Church, which I visited.

Steps led to a woodland path, which descended to follow the creek until I reached a point where there are open views along the coast. I walked to the lighthouse over open downland. The lighthouse is now a holiday let.

Portscatho was hidden from view until I passed by a lovely path-side garden with a cancer charity box for those who wanted to give to appreciate the lovely garden. Then around the corner there was Portscatho – once a fishing village, but now a quiet resort.

Portscatho to Portloe

Date: August bank holiday
Distance: 7.4 miles
Grade: strenuous
Weather: the hottest day of the year with no breeze and no shade!

Sometimes I feel I push myself to the limit – on this day, in that heat, I felt I pushed myself well beyond the limit!

I started my walk at the point where I had left off the previous walk, at Portscatho, with its narrow lanes by the beach and harbour club. There were lovely cottages with colourful bedding plants.

The walk was very undulating, looking down on crowded beaches. The bay curved to reveal the coastline ahead to Nare Head.

The path later led to a narrow road by the back of Nare Hotel and Carne Beach, where because of the brilliant weather the beach was crowded, as was the narrow lane, blocked by cars.

Shortly afterwards, however, steps took me back to the coast path, where I negotiated a steep descent followed by a steep ascent near the steps down to the beach at Porthcurnick and later past an old fisherman's cottage.

The ascent to reach Nare Head was very steep. With the hot sun and no breeze, there was no shade.

Normally when climbing a hill or steps if I am beginning to get tired I will count fifty footsteps before I stop for a breather. That day was so hot I was having to stop after fifteen steps! Help!

I met quite a number of friendly walkers as I struggled to the top of Nare Head, all struggling!

The climb is tough, but the views are a reward, both towards Gull Rock and back over where I had walked – the Lizard looked a long way behind!

Undulating paths eventually led into the small steep village of Portloe by the side of the Lugger Inn.

Due to cramp all evening and during the night, I decided not to walk the next day.

Portloe to East Portholland

Distance: about 3 miles

Much of the route led through thick bracken before I met two workmen using strimmers to cut the bracken down. From then on it was easier. However, the start of the walk went down between an old boathouse and a chapel, both converted into houses. The views back over Portloe were beautiful, as were the gardens.

The walk was much easier than the previous walk, and

continued to reach, first, West Portholland and, after a short road walk, East Portholland, a tiny hamlet.

As I had no phone signal, someone dropping off her husband, who was also a walker, kindly took me back to my campsite at Veryan. I have met such lovely helpful people on my walks.

East Portholland to Gorran Haven

Date: 1 September 2017
Weather: changeable!

A day never to be forgotten!

Due to the hot weather and my strenuous walk on Nare Head a few days before, and with good weather forecast, I did something which I later regretted. There are three cardinal things walkers should never do, even on a sunny day.

1. Never go without waterproofs.

2. Never remove the thick plastic liner from one's rucksack.

3. Never, when walking alone, remove the survival bag (mine is quite a heavy gauge) from one's rucksack.

I plead guilty to all three.

Well, it was a lovely day when I set out. Then, just after admiring the setting of Caerhays Castle by Porthluney Cove, the black clouds started rolling in. The sky opened and the rain came down in stair rods as I left a small woodland, turning the steep grass-based path into a mudslide – a treacherous, slippery slide. My feet were slipping and sliding in all directions. I could easily have fallen heavily and needed my survival bag. Lesson learned! Never go walking alone on a coast path without a survival bag. As I was soaking-wet, hypothermia would have soon set in. I was soaked through to my bra and pants, my shorts, blouse, socks, walking boots –

and I could have wrung the water out of my sun hat!

My map turned into papier mâché; and with my head down against the rain, I missed several of the acorn signs, so had to retrace my steps on several occasions, taking even longer!

I found myself on a narrow steep-sided lane above Hemmick Beach before climbing up to Dodman Point. The path was quite steep in places, levelling out and then rising quite steeply to reach a huge granite cross erected in memory of the many sailors who had been shipwrecked on the rocks below, and maybe as a warning marker for future sailors. It is said the name Dodman is sadly a corruption of 'deadman'.

For a short while the rain moved away and I was able to take a photograph of the massive cross; but as I left, the rain started again with a vengeance!

My friend, worrying about me, kept phoning me, and each time I had to take my rucksack off to get my phone out to answer it – I was not sure if it was safe to use in the pouring rain! I found the contents of my rucksack were soaked. My phone was in a case, but the £10 and £20 notes in my wallet were soaked. The new £5 notes, I discovered, really are washable!

I trudged on, eventually reaching the lanes of Gorran Haven, formerly a busy fishing village, where the rainwater was running down each side of the road to the beach. Thankfully I was being picked up – no taxi would have been willing to take such a soaking-wet passenger back to her campsite!

We have had a lot of laughs over it since, but it was not funny at the time. Never have I ever been so wet!

Cornwall's weather is unpredictable!

The large cross erected on Dodman Point.

Gorran Haven to Pentewan

Leaving the narrow lanes of Gorran Haven I found beautiful houses with beautiful sea views over the little harbour. The path leaves the houses behind and follows the coastline after crossing a small wooden bridge and a stile into a field to reach the cliffs. The path continues past Chapel Point, then over a driveway, continuing to follow the path to Portmellon. I followed the road uphill and down through a park to enter Mevagissey. Steps descend to the harbour. Mevagissey has a very pretty harbour and it was crowded on such a lovely day.

Apparently, the name Mevagissey originates from two saints, St Mevan and St Issey. In days gone by, Mevagissey was a well-known pilchard port, but now it is more well known for the tourist industry.

The path goes around the harbour to climb steeply up across a playing area to a flight of ninety steps and across fields to drop down by a beautiful beach and the enormous campsite of Pentewan Holiday Park. Then it joins the road for a short distance before turning right into the pretty village of Pentewan, with its old harbour.

Pentewan has a small square surrounded by cottages with lovely flower boxes and hanging baskets.

Pentewan to Par

Date: April 2018
Grade – strenuous.

By this stage of the walk I was eighty-three was my first coastal walk after the winter. It soon showed me who was boss! It soon also told me I wasn't as fit as I thought I was! I later worked out that there were approximately 376 steps down and 207 steps up, totalling 583, and I felt like collapsing by the time I reached the picturesque harbour of Charlestown.

Charlestown, with its old sailing ships in its harbour, is often used in films. It is so named after a man called Charles Rashleigh, a businessman whose family, over several generations, did so much for the port and area. They were involved in the china-clay industry, filling cargo ships with clay and porcelain to be exported all over the world.

I visited the Shipwreck Museum on the harbourside before continuing the walk to Par. That part of the walk is quite level to the lovely Carlyon Bay beach, passing in front of the Carlyon Bay Hotel and keeping to the seaward side of the golf course towards the china-clay works. Here the walk becomes more industrial, following the works perimeter fence and later running alongside the railway to join a busy road. I passed under a railway bridge, over a level crossing, under another rail arch, into the village of Par and, later, on to Par Sands.

The lovely colours of this cove between Pentewan and Charlestown.

Charlestown Harbour, Cornwall, often used in films.

Par to the Polrun Ferry

Distance: 7 miles

This walk goes out to Gribbin Head and later passes through the very narrow lanes of Fowey to finish at the harbour. Being a Sunday, there were quite a lot of walkers at the start of this walk, but judging from snippets of conversation I rather think that many were doing the walk en route to have their lunch at the tiny harbour of Polkerris, where there is another pub named after the Rashleigh family.

Polkerris, although quiet now, was once another busy fishing port for pilchards. The original lifeboat station – now moved to Fowey – is now a beach shop and café.

Trinity House erected the daymark on Gribbin Head – now owned by the National Trust. It is eighty-four feet tall and red and white, and can be seen for miles. Nearby is Daphne Du Maurier's one time home at Menabilly. She used her house as a basic idea for Manderley in *Rebecca*. It was built originally by the Rashleigh family – again!

The coast path drops down from the daymark, and for a short distance there is a series of stepping stones between a little lake and the shore.

Fowey, pronounced Foy, is approached along the part-wooded estuary side, with the ruin of Catherine's Castle nearby. The path drops down to the intriguingly named Readymoney Cove. Today Fowey is a china-clay port and a holiday resort – and the ferry port (foot ferry) to go over to Polruan – but the port has a very turbulent history in centuries past.

I caught a bus part way back and walked the rest of the way back to my campsite overlooking St Austell Bay near Par.

The car ferry to Polruan is further up the River Fowey.

The foot ferry between Fowey and Polruan.

Polruan to Polperro

Distance: 7.1 miles
Weather: fine
Grade: strenuous

For some reason I chose to do this walk from Polruan to Polperro the day after the hard walk from Pentewan to Charlestown – possibly as Trish, my niece, was going to walk with me, and I thought it would be more scenic than the industrial section around Par.

We had a great day in good weather; but, with another 218 steps down and 306 steps up, making 524 in total, this meant over the two days I walked up or down over 1,000 steps! It was a very scenic walk.

Starting with the foot ferry to Polruan from Fowey, we then climbed up to a grassy area owned by the National Trust. From there was a lovely view of Fowey, Polruan and the estuary. There was a stiff climb before Pencarrow Head, which passes the isolated Watch House – the only habitable house for miles. Lansallos Church is set a bit inland. There is an obelisk beside the path that is a daymark to warn shipping of the dangers of a submerged Udder Rock, whose bell makes a mournful sound.

After many more ups and downs the path approaches the almost hidden inlet of Polperro.

Following the waymarked path, we arrived at a rocky lookout point, where there was a beautiful drystone wall. We then descended on a narrow path, admiring the quaint houses, rooftops and narrow streets below.

Polperro is very picturesque and often features on calendars.

We ended the day with a lovely meal.

Polperro to West Looe

Distance: 5 miles

This walk I also did with Trish, and – an unexpected surprise – Matthew, Trish's son, arrived as we were setting off.

The coast path started by crossing a narrow stone bridge among the narrow lanes of picturesque Polperro. As we climbed the steps, a lovely view over the entrance of the harbour opened up. A little further along the cliff path we were surprised to find the War Memorial Cross. It is situated in a lovely position on National Trust land between Polperro and Talland.

It was mainly easy downland walking with lovely views.

On a clear day Eddystone Lighthouse can be seen.

The path descends towards Talland Bay and then climbs back up to the cliff edge.

We also saw an adder sunning itself on the path, and I was able to photograph it.

The path eventually arrived at a suburban road at Hannafore – the west end of East Looe – overlooking the island offshore known either as Looe Island or St George's Island, now a nature reserve.

It is a useful road to know about as car parking is free all day. Matthew had left his car there and kindly took us back to our cars.

West Looe to Seaton

Distance: 5 miles

West and East Looe are joined together by a seven-arched bridge spanning the river, with West Looe on one side of the river and East Looe on the other. Centuries ago they used to be two separate towns, each apparently sending an MP to Parliament. One side was known as the money side, and the other the sunny side!

I left my camper van on the roadside at West Looe (free all day) and set off following the promenade, and then a short distance of road, before I reached the riverside. I could see a lot of boats in the harbour, especially towards the mouth of the river, as I crossed the seven-arched bridge to walk along the harbourside on the other side.

The path climbs steeply above the harbour and then through scrubland and eventually comes out by the Bay View Caravan Site, and later the Woolly Monkey Sanctuary, before going through woodland and eventually down a steep lane to the beach at Seaton.

I returned to Looe by the lanes (another five miles) to reach my camper van at West Looe.

Seaton to Tregantle Fort

Distance: about 7 miles

Unfortunately the tide was in at Seaton so I had to walk up the steps and narrow road to Downderry – a densely built elongated village with houses and bungalows on its steep sides. At low tide it is possible, by going down a narrow slipway, to cut along the beach.

The walk continued along the road until halfway round a steep hairpin bend, where a fingerpost directed me right. The path then zigzagged steeply upwards through scrubland, and then levelled out a bit before descending to a road at the western end of the seafront at Portwrinkle.

At the other end of the village there was a café, where I stopped for a coffee.

The path continued for a short way up the tarmac road before turning up a signposted path, which then climbed steeply and reached the edge of the golf course.

At the further end of the golf course was the Tregantle Firing Range. Being August, the path through the firing range was open, but somehow I missed a footpath sign – and on a firing range one doesn't go 'off-piste'! I decided it would be safer to follow the acorn signs, which took me to a path behind a roadside hedge, before I had to walk along the roadside. The path eventually turned right into the coastal road. The road followed the border fence of Tregantle Fort, and then a path went through more scrubland before joining the road again opposite the Sharrow Car Park, where I was going to be picked up.

Not the best of walks!

Tregantle was one of a chain of forts built around Plymouth to protect the important Royal Naval Dockyard – some former forts in the area have since been converted into apartments.

Tregantle Fort to Cawsand

My niece, Trish, joined me to do this next section, leaving her car at the Sharrow Car Park. We were amazed at the number of wooden chalets built on the slopes overlooking Whitsand Bay. I believe they were built just after the war, when Plymouth had been so heavily bombed. Now most of them appear to be holiday homes or weekend retreats.

We followed the signed path, part of it going between the chalets, part on the road, until we reached an official fingerpost stating the miles to Rame Head and Cawsand. The path took us down through scrubland, where I managed to trip over, banging my glasses against my face, resulting later in a black eye and a small cut. Trish, being a nurse, patched me up!

The path came out on a tarmac drive down to another fort – now a wedding venue – with beautiful roadside poppies.

After crossing the venue access road the path climbed to reach the headland going towards Rame Head. There were lovely views back over Whitsand Bay. Ponies were grazing on the headland and a few families were enjoying picnics.

The path was across open downland, in scorching heat and again no shade (2018 being the hottest summer in living memory!).

Rame Head Chapel is situated on the top of a steep hill.

As the path turns inland, the views over Plymouth Sound come into view.

A good cliff path then goes to Penlee Point and starts to descend through woodland to eventually come out in the little harbour town of Cawsand.

We had originally intended to continue through the adjoining harbour of Kingsand and the Mount Edgcumbe Country Park to Cremyll, where my camper van was parked. But we were both exhausted with the heat, so, after a drink for both of us, we decided on a taxi back to my camper van.

We enjoyed a meal at the Edgcumbe Arms, sitting in the sunshine overlooking Plymouth Sound with a view over the city of Plymouth, watching the many boats of all kinds going past. The Cremyll foot ferry, alongside the pub, has been operating for over 200 years.

Cawsand to the Plymouth Ferry

Distance: 3.5 miles

I was dropped off near Kingsand – the lanes were so narrow they are best avoided! – and I walked through the village to Cawsand's square, where I had finished the previous walk with Trish. It was a shame we couldn't have gone further together as it turned out to be a lovely walk.

It is difficult to know where Cawsand ends and Kingsand begins as they are joined at the hip, so to speak – in fact there is a sign saying Devon/Cornwall as in years past Cawsand was in Cornwall and Kingsand in Devon!

There were quaint cottages with lovely colourful window boxes. The narrow lanes are too narrow for most vehicles.

Climbing up a narrow lane I found a fingerpost and a wide gate on the right with a notice saying Mount Edgcumbe Country Park – beyond it I could see a wide level carriage drive.

The view across Plymouth Sound and the surrounding area was beautiful in such lovely weather.

The path was easy to follow and later went up through beech trees. It must be a lovely walk in autumn.

This is all part of the Mount Edgcumbe Country Park, given to Plymouth City Council for the use of the people of Plymouth and the general public. It also has formal gardens and it has the National Collection of Camellias.

The path eventually dropped down to the water's edge, passing several follies, and later the path went through part of the beautiful gardens with colourful flower beds and a pavilion where refreshments were being served. There is also a deer park there with a viewing seat to take in the fabulous view extending to the Tamar Bridge, the whole city of Plymouth, Plymouth Sound and several estuaries and far beyond.

Plymouth to the Laira Bridge (A379)

After taking the ferry across the Tamar to the slipway at Admiral's Hard, I turned right and later right again to reach the Royal William Yard, which once housed the naval buildings but more recently has been developed into prestigious apartments and offices. The offices include the new home (2019) of the South West Coast Path Association – just yards from the coast path.

My first surprise was to have to climb the Eric Wallis Memorial Steps to Devil's Point Park, sometimes referred to as the stairway to Devon, which later looked out on Drake's Island.

I then followed my Plymouth Waterfront Walkway leaflet past the Royal Marines barracks, Millbay Road and Millbay Docks,

62

and walked along the promenade below the Hoe and Smeaton's Tower, the iconic red-and-white lighthouse.

Being May bank holiday Sunday, the pavements were heaving with families, pushchairs, dogs on leads, etc. – not making for quick walking!

Later I passed the Barbican and walked around Sutton Harbour with its pavement cafés, etc. I didn't cheat and go across the ferry from the Mayflower Steps to the ferry point at Mountbatten, but continued past the marine aquarium and later through the industrial area around Cattedown Wharf.

Whilst not an area of outstanding beauty, I found it interesting for its tall red-and-white South West Coast Path pillar as well as a similar-sized one, laid lengthways, forming a seat. The unusual red-and-white iron South West Coast Path signs are unique to Plymouth.

I later walked along Finnigan Road to reach Laira Bridge and the A379 on the Plymouth to Plymstock road, where I was able to catch a bus back to Devonport. Then I took the ferry back to my camper van, parked at Cremyll Ferry Car Park (where all-day parking was a lot cheaper than parking all day in Plymouth!).

The horizontal South West Coast Path sign and seat on the outskirts of Plymouth, in the industrial area between Cattedown Road and the new Laira Bridge (A379).

Two unusual South West Coast Path signs unique to Plymouth,

Laira Bridge to the Noss Mayo Ferry

Date: May
Distance: 7.3 miles
Grade: easy

Well, I often finish my walks feeling a wreck, but not long after I started this walk at Laira Bridge, following the wrought-iron cut-out fingerposts, I was looking at a wreck washed up on an inlet by Hooe Lake.

From Hooe Lake I went through a wooded area until I reached the older colourful houses and pubs before a large new housing development being built overlooking a yachting marina that reminded me of the marinas in Auckland Harbour in New Zealand.

Then I passed the Mountbatten ferry point and climbed to the top of Jenny Cliff, which has views over Plymouth Sound and the islands offshore. The path ran along the cliff edge before disappearing down new steps and through a bluebell wood. Then I rounded a bend and saw Bovisand Bay, with its lovely chalet park with uninterrupted sea views.

The path was easy going.

Later the Great Mew Stone became the focal point. I passed Wembury Church perched on the high cliff overlooking Wembury Beach.

Beyond the church the path continued easy going to reach Rocket House, and later the ferry at Warren Point to cross the Yealm Estuary.

The trouble with the south coast is the number of estuaries that have to be crossed, some with limited crossings. One – the Erme (near Bigbury) – has no ferry or bridge, so you must either cross at low tide at your peril or (as I did) finish one day on one side of the estuary and start the next day on the other side.

The ferry at Warren Point operates three ways over the River Yealm and its tributary Newton Creek, so Warren Point is linked with both Newton Ferrers and Noss Mayo. For the coast path the link between Warren Point and Noss Mayo is needed.

Noss Mayo to the Erme Estuary

Distance: 8 miles

Noss Mayo is the point on the other side of the ferry link from Warren Point.

I was given a lift to Noss Mayo and I walked along the jetty. I was surprised to see a sign saying 'Drop This To Call Ferry' on a dark round piece of timber. A person who manned the river taxi appeared and took me to the other side, charging me £3.50. I was the only passenger.

The path led up through bluebell woods to a point where there were open views back along the coast to Wembury Church and the Great Mew Stone. Gorse, thrift, bluebells and larks singing overhead – what bliss! It was easy walking.

Later I found a holiday village with static caravans tucked away in a bay as well as a fingerpost reading 'Noss Mayo 5.5 miles' and, in the other direction, 'Mothercombe 3 miles'.

Passing by a pillbox I came to a granite seat surrounded by a carpet of bluebells. It was placed there for a beautiful view. About a mile further on, the easy part finished and the strenuous part started! A steep descent was followed by a steep ascent to St Anchorite's Rock. Near here I remember meeting a small group of teenagers – obviously not regular walkers, as one of them said to me, "Is it like this all the way?"

I didn't have the heart to say yes! The path then went down to Bugle Hole, and then steps zigzagged up through bluebells.

Later the wide Erme Estuary came into view, finishing with steps down to the beach, which was quite crowded. The path turned inland, past the beach car park, where I was being picked up.

The Erme Estuary to Bigbury-on-Sea

Distance: 5 miles

A few months after walking to the Erme Estuary I camped on a farm site in Bigbury. Lovely views; lovely day! I had arrived during the afternoon. It was such a beautiful day, I thought, 'Go for it, gal!' I then decided to walk it in reverse, from Bigbury-on-Sea to the Erme Estuary, that day instead of waiting for the next day – good choice!

In one book I had read as follows: 'some very steep gradients on the first mile which might be beyond the capabilities of the elderly or inexperienced'!

All right, then, that didn't include me! At eighty-two, I was not elderly – I was old! And I didn't regard myself as inexperienced!

I set out and walked to the Challaborough Holiday Village – very undulating, but there were beautiful views all around the coast. Then I reached the high point of Beacon Point, which has extensive views inland to Dartmoor. From here the path dropped steeply down to follow the eastern side of the estuary, opposite where I had reached on my last walk. I decided instead of retracing my steps, and seeing the same views, that I would make it into a circular walk (that's the beauty of carrying a map at all times). The path wound its way up through woodland, across both pasture and fields of cereal crops, then through lanes to reach the quaint hamlet of Kingston. I had a coffee in the pub, talking to other walkers there. The hamlet has several beautiful thatched cottages.

Walking along the very narrow lanes I made my way back to the Challaborough Holiday Village, then on coastal path back to Bigbury and my campsite. I had walked about ten miles in total.

By 5.30 a.m. terrible gales had blown in, rocking my camper van from side to side, and it poured with rain all the next day, so I was pleased I had decided to walk the previous day in glorious weather. Otherwise the warning in that book, 'beyond the capabilities of the elderly', might have proved correct!

Bigbury-on-Sea to the Bantham Ferry

Distance: 2.7 miles

I love Bigbury-on-Sea with Burgh Island lying just offshore. At high tide the island is cut off, but there is a special sea tractor which takes people to and from the island. There is an art-deco hotel on the island, and the island often features on calendars. Guests to the hotel, it has been said, have included Agatha Christie, Edward, Prince of Wales (briefly King Edward VIII) and a certain Wallis Simpson.

The short walk to the Bantham ferry I had intended to do at the end of my walk from Hope Cove (which I had walked the previous year), but I had missed the ferry (only available for an hour) due to the tide. Leaving my farm campsite, I walked first through farmland and then through low-lying estuary gravel to the ferry point and returned the same way.

The beach at Bigbury-on-Sea with Burgh Island in the distance.

Bantham to Hope Cove

Distance: 3 miles

What a nightmare! Another day never to be forgotten!

I left the campsite at Slapton Sands, where I was staying at 7.30 a.m., taking two buses to reach Hope Cove. First I caught a double-decker to Kingsbridge, then a single-decker to Hope Cove. Going at that time of morning, I was not eligible for free travel either! I arrived at Hope Cove and set off westward towards Bigbury-on-Sea so full of energy! But it was so unbelievably hot it took me longer than planned to reach the Avon Estuary ferry at Bantham. The ferry is only available for one hour as it is tidal. I just missed it! I decided then to retrace my steps past Thurlestone Rock (a large rock with a hole in it) to Hope Cove. Unfortunately I just missed the lunchtime bus back to the campsite and I then had to wait until 6.15 p.m. in intense heat for the next bus! I even tried to find a cool church to sit in – but there was no church! I tried the chapel, but the doors were locked. I went into the pub for a lunch that I didn't really need as I had a packed lunch with me, just for some shade! However, there is a limit to the time a woman can stay in a pub on her own!

I eventually caught the bus at 6.15 p.m., but my troubles were not yet over. On the way to Kingsbridge a car had broken down in the narrow lanes and was being loaded on to a long-based breakdown truck, so of course there was a delay. Eventually we arrived in Kingsbridge Bus Station just in time to see the back of the double-decker bus that I needed to catch disappearing out of the bus station. I had missed it by a few seconds. Oh well, it just wasn't my day! I eventually got back to my campsite at 8.15 p.m., having walked only three miles of path and three miles back, and I got sunburnt for my troubles.

The next day I'm afraid I had an R & R day. No, Hope Cove does nothing for me – I can't think why!

Hope Cove to the East Portlemouth Ferry

Distance: 8 miles

Staying at Slapton Sands Campsite again, I took two buses to Hope Cove, leaving, as before, at 7.30 a.m. On reaching Hope Cove, I walked into the village square at Inner Hope to see the cluster of thatched cottages, then walked to the left of the beach out to Bolt Tail, with its extensive views back over Hope Cove and beyond. Somehow it reminded me of Skomer in Pembrokeshire, with its high downland and rocky coastline (minus the puffins, of course). This section is described as probably the most spectacular high-cliff walk on this coast.

The rock formations from Bolt Tail eastwards differ from those to the west.

The going becomes steep with a sharp descent to Soar Mill Cove and an equally exacting gradient up the other side. Once past Soar Mill Cove the walk becomes easier along the cliff edge to Bolt Head. The path then turns left and becomes a beautiful cliff-hugging path overlooking Starehole Bay, ending in steps cut out of the rocky pinnacles, beautiful on such a lovely day.

I saw carpets of thrift and the first heathers of the season.

The path then went through woodland to reach South Sands and North Sands for an estuary-side walk and on through the narrow streets of Salcombe to yet another ferry point, to Portlemouth.

There are some delightful buildings along Fore Street, the main street.

The now ruined Salcombe Castle (or Fort Charles, as it is sometimes known) was built by Henry VIII.

Salcombe has hotels and a youth hostel.

I caught a bus back to Kingsbridge and another bus back to my campsite at Slapton Sands.

East Portlemouth to Start Point Lighthouse

Distance: about 9 miles
Weather: brilliant sunshine
Grade: strenuous

This walk was beautiful, with bluebells, bluebells and more bluebells!

I was dropped off at Mill Bay, where two ladies with their dogs directed me to the start of the coastal path at Ferry Point, East Portlemouth. I walked through the bluebell woods overlooking the estuary with occasional views over to Salcombe.

This walk will always be remembered by me for a number of things – the carpets of bluebells, primroses, thrift/sea pinks and gorse, the lovely weather, and the pleasure of meeting a couple of people I knew.

As I rounded a rocky headland miles from anywhere, I recognised two members of our church, Dave and Ginny – it's a small world! Dave asked if I minded him taking a photograph of Ginny and me. I guessed the photograph would get back to where I live before I did – and it sure did! to mutual friends of ours!

Thankfully, that day I wasn't wearing shorts, which I only wear when I'm not with people I know!

Later on I passed Prawle Coastguard Station, which was followed by a low-level section, then a rocky climb to where Start Point Lighthouse came into view.

I will always remember this rocky section carpeted with bluebells. It was an excellent walk in brilliant sunshine.

I walked to Start Point Lighthouse and then further on to the car park, where I was being picked up. Here many primroses were still in flower and I noted the fingerpost stating 'Poole 168 miles'!

Start Point Lighthouse to Torcross

Date: July
Weather: fine

It was a fantastically clear day with views the whole way around Start Bay from Start Point to Torcross, Slapton Sands and the entrance to Dartmouth Harbour.

I parked in the Start Point car park and I set out hoping to walk to Torcross and back. The start of the walk was downhill along a narrow path through bracken. A windswept apple tree formed an arch over the path. Further on, I read the sad noticeboards relating the tragedy of the now deserted Hallsands hamlet. I viewed and took photographs of several cottages hanging dangerously over the cliff edge. This tragedy came about mainly due to the excessive dredging of gravel to construct the Devonport Dockyard. Subsequently torrential storms caused flooding and cliff falls, making the cottages uninhabitable. Further on (and back from the edge) were a number of modern houses, mainly holiday cottages.

Wooden steps bordered by wild poppies led down to a quiet beach with a few upturned boats pulled up on to the beach. At the beach end, the path climbed into meadows of wild flowers busy with butterflies, and swallows and skylarks flew overhead.

Further on the path dropped down among the cottages of Beesands, the hamlet consisting of a string of cottages, a pub, a small chapel, a fish-and-chip café and an ice-cream outlet, where I bought myself an ice cream.

Beesands has a long road and a beach, at the end of which the coastal path continues beyond the last house. The path climbs up behind the house, then up a flight of steps through woodland on to an open downland area before dropping down again by cottages and a pub at Torcross, where a lovely view opens up.

I had viewed footage of the storms of February 2014 on Youtube: the cottages' windows were blown in and the waves were crashing over the roofs of the cottages. Now the cottages looked spick and span after being newly decorated outside, and the sea was very calm.

The walk back to Start Point Lighthouse to get my camper van was hot. Worse still were the horseflies. I was bitten on the inside of my right elbow, and whilst I was hitting that one another bit my left calf, and as I hit that one off another bit me on my left thumb! Thank you very much – I scratched all night! Next July I must remember to come prepared, I thought. It brought back memories of the horseflies in Cornwall the previous July!

In the evening I walked from the campsite, along the beach to the Torcross pub, renowned for its fish and chips, and back to the campsite, adding a mile and a half to my day's walk.

Torcross to the Kingswear Ferry

Distance: 10 miles

Early the next morning (before the horseflies were awake!) I walked from the campsite to join the coast path by the Slapton Sands War Memorial to walk to Dartmouth via Strete.

When I reached the end of Slapton Sands beach, I walked up a wide track, then climbed the new steep wooded zigzag path and steps, which emerge much nearer the hotel in Strete than the previous path did. Then after competing with the traffic on the steep hill I stopped to photograph a lovely newly built drystone wall.

The views back over Slapton Sands and Slapton Ley were magnificent on such a lovely morning. The freshwater Leys are of great interest to birdwatchers. Here waterfowl, both resident and migratory, can be observed among the reeds and rushes.

The path went seaward after Strete, crossing fields where cattle were grazing. The views were of the obelisk ahead and small offshore islands I would pass on the next section of my walk. The path then curved back towards the road, with a steep downhill path followed by a steep uphill section to cross the main road. The path led through another large herd of cattle with calves, then down a track to enter another field,

73

overlooking the beautiful Blackpool Sands.

The path then went over a narrow stone bridge by a large house being rethatched. Crossing the road opposite the entrance to Blackpool Sands, the path wound its way through the roadside woodland to emerge on the road. It then crossed to a steep lane, which eventually came out in Stoke Fleming's narrow streets. I walked through more woodland adjoining a park, and crossed the main road into a straight, narrow high-banked lane, and arrived at a National Trust car park before going seaward again. Then I found myself in a deep valley and arrived on to a low cliff at the entrance of the Dart Estuary.

I stopped for a coffee at the café at Dart Castle and then visited the riverside church of St Petrox, a Celtic saint. I then followed the Dart along narrow quayside lanes decorated with colourful window boxes before reaching the centre of Dartmouth.

Dartmouth, with all its sailing boats on the River Dart, the cafés, holidaymakers and the gorgeous weather, looked quite continental, especially with Kingswear with its terraced houses on the other side of the River Dart.

I returned to Slapton on the front seat of a double-decker, taking in all the lovely coastal scenery. A wonderful day!

Although Slapton Sands looks very peaceful now, it has not always been so. On 13 November 1943, villagers including farmers, in the village of Slapton and in several other villages nearby, were given six weeks' notice to pack up everything they owned, including livestock, and move outside the area, which was to be requisitioned for D-Day practice. Seven hundred and fifty people in all were evacuated by 29 December 1943.

Sadly the D-Day rehearsals are remembered for one terrible disaster when German U-boats attacked a practice convoy and over 700 US servicemen were killed in one night. The monument on the beach was erected to commemorate the locals' sacrifice.

A salvaged American Sherman tank stands as a memorial at the Torcross end of Slapton Sands. It is often surrounded by wreaths of poppies.

Kingswear to Brixham

Distance: 10.8 miles
Weather: beautiful
Grade: strenuous

I had a lift to Dartmouth and then caught the 9.30-a.m. ferry from Dartmouth to Kingswear. On reaching the Kingswear side, I started the walk by passing under an arch and climbing the steep Alma steps to a single-track road that led to woodland. I climbed down some steep steps and up more steps through bluebell woods to eventually reach a lookout and an old World War Two searchlight station at Froward Point.

There were ponies grazing nearby; bluebells, primroses and gorse were in bloom. The path opened out and there was spectacular scenery in spectacular weather!

Further along the path I came to Pudcombe Cove, where I was more than a little surprised to see my friend Cyril (who had given me a lift to the Kingswear ferry). He was visiting the National Trust house and gardens at Coleton Fishacre, which, unknown to me, stretched down to Pudcombe Cove. Whilst waiting for me to arrive, he had told several people standing by him that at eighty-two I was walking the entire South West Coast Path, and I arrived to a round of applause!

Hard enough so far, but on reaching Scabbacombe Head and Sands the hard work really began! Up, up, up the path went, and then down again to Man Sands, with its large pebble beach, followed by the climb to the top of the 420-foot Southdown Cliff. The path levelled out to soft downland to reach Sharkham Point.

The coast curved around at that point to St Mary's Bay, on the outskirts of Brixham, south-west of Berry Head, where I was being picked up.

Another of the unusual South West Coast Path signs.

Brixham to Paignton

I caught a train from my campsite at Dawlish Warren to Paignton and then caught a double-decker bus – front seat, of course! – to Brixham. Finding the coast path, I walked via Berry Head to St Mary's Bay, where I had finished my walk the previous year. I then returned to Brixham Harbour, where there were boats of all sizes at anchor, including the full-size replica of Sir Francis Drake's ship the *Golden Hind*, which he sailed around the world from 1577 to 1580.

Passing the fish warehouses I walked around the edge of the harbour to the delightful Churston Cove. Climbing out of Churston Cove I walked up a steep, narrow zigzag path over the rocks, then through bluebell woods and along beside the fence of the Churston Golf Course.

Later I arrived at Broadsands Beach, where the path turns inland to go under the Torbay Steam Railway bridge. Turning right up a flight of steps, the path runs alongside the railway line as far as Goodrington Sands.

Crossing the sandy beach, I walked up the zigzag gardens to Paignton. I had last walked up this path sixty-plus years ago!

I ended the day's walk at Paignton Pier, and then caught the train back from Paignton to Dawlish.

A replica of Sir Francis Drake's Golden Hind, *permanently moored in Brixham Harbour.*

Paignton to Babbacombe

I took the train again to Paignton and walked to the pier, where I had finished my walk the day before. As I was walking towards Torquay, I passed a B & B or hotel called The One Lost Sock!

The path continued across a park before coming out on the main road midway between Paignton and Torquay. The tide was out, so I was able to walk across the beach on the outskirts of Torquay.

I walked around the harbour with its many boats and turned right at the Imperial Hotel on to the signed coast path, reaching an open area at Daddyhole Plain. Later the path descends to the seafront road at Meadfoot Beach. The cliff path goes around Thatcher's Point to Hope's Nose. Crossing the road, the path then goes up on to the top of a raised bank parallel to the road. The side of the bank was covered in blue and white bluebells. Dropping down to the level of the road, a sign directs the footpath down the Bishop's Walk towards Anstey's Cove. The path later enters woods and a signpost points the way to Babbacombe and St Mary's Church.

I followed the headland round to find a coast-path sign directing me through another woodland. Here I was able to take a photograph of a lovely orchid.

Later I reached a hotel overlooking the beach. I went over a wooden bridge to Oddicombe Beach and the Cliff Railway. Be warned, there are 261 steps to climb! I know – I climbed them! After a long day's walking, I looked at the steps and nearly gave up the will to live. Yes, I could have gone up the Cliff Railway in two minutes, but I didn't cheat!

It was only when I reached the top and was waiting for a bus to take me back to my camper van that I realised that I had left my walking pole on a bench halfway up the steps, where I had stopped for a breather. But I just didn't have the energy to go back down – and walk back up again! I wonder where it is now?

Babbacombe to the Teignmouth Ferry

Distance: 6.4 miles
Weather: dry and very humid

Sometime later I camped at a farm site overlooking the River Teign at Shaldon, and caught a bus to where I had finished my walk at Babbacombe. On this occasion I descended the steps at the side of the cliff railway, walking by the bench where I had left my walking pole on the previous occasion!

The path went through overgrown bracken, brambles and some nettles, then at the top of the slope it came out on to the main road, only to turn right down a side road back to join the path through woodland.

This section was the only section so far that I didn't enjoy. Due to the amount of woodland I felt vulnerable as I was unable to see far ahead and I thought my mobile phones would probably not have a signal if I needed to use them. (I always carry two phones on different networks.)

I was near the sea, but unable to see it for trees. The path was very undulating and steep in places, ending in a very steep descent into Shaldon, with views overlooking Teignmouth.

From the embarkation point of the Teignmouth ferry I went back to my camper van, parked in a Shaldon car park. My heart missed a beat when I saw a notice stuck to my windscreen. 'Oh no, not a parking fine!' I thought. 'That's all I need after a hard day's walk.' Instead it was a note to say, 'If you are interested in selling this camper van, please phone number -------'!

That happens two or three times a year. My camper van is twenty-three years old! I always have a good feeling when others admire it! I drove back to the campsite with a smile on my face.

Teignmouth to Dawlish

From the campsite at Dawlish Warren I walked to the railway station at Dawlish, turned right and walked along the beach, then along the wide sea wall to Teignmouth – walking parallel to the railway line that runs along the edge of the beach between the sea and the beautiful red cliffs. This railway line from Teignmouth to Starcross is the one that has been washed away on numerous occasions, including during the winter storms of 2014.

Reaching Teignmouth, I found a nice coffee shop and then returned by train to my campsite at Dawlish Warren.

Dawlish to the Exmouth Ferry

I arrived at Dawlish Warren campsite late in the afternoon and decided to walk from the site to Dawlish Railway Station and to the Exmouth ferry at Starcross. The ferry operates in summer; I believe in winter there is a long diversion up the Exe to Topsham.

Exmouth to Budleigh Salterton

October 2014
Distance: 5.5 miles

Two and a half years after walking with the group from the Lizard to Helford and (where I left the group) I met up with them again for a special birthday reunion at Exmouth, which the remainder of the group had reached on their walk of the South West Coast Path.

The group consisted of Lionel and Gaynor, Kathy, Mel, John, Jo, Jennifer and me, meeting to celebrate the special birthdays of Jo, Jennifer, Kathy, Gaynor and myself.

I joined them on the Friday and we enjoyed an excellent meal at the Beacon Hill Hotel at Exmouth. We were joined by Kathy on the Saturday morning and set off wearing waterproofs. Less than two and a half miles later, the sun came out as we walked to the end of Exmouth's sandy beach. I was surprised to see a number of camper vans which had obviously spent the night parked along the beach road.

The first stop was to admire the Silver Pointed Monument (opened by Prince Charles), marking the most westerly and the oldest part of the Jurassic Coast.

It was easy walking on the clifftop before dropping down through a massive caravan park, which has been renamed the Devon Cliffs Holiday Park. We, as a family, knew it years ago as a farm camping site and first camped there in the late sixties. It was then known as Sandy Bay Campsite. We walked in front of the Beach Café and above the beach, up and around the edge of the camp, where a beautiful view opened up – steep red cliffs in the foreground stretching along to Budleigh Salterton and beyond to Sidmouth and Lyme Regis. After stopping for coffee/snacks we took a deep breath and climbed to the top of the red cliffs, later dropping down to a wide path overlooking Budleigh Salterton with its pebble beach, boats, etc. We stopped for another coffee break at a lovely clean small beachside café. It was the end of our walk after we had walked to the Otter Estuary Nature Reserve, at the end of the beach.

We walked back through the small town of Budleigh Salterton, where we caught the bus back to Exmouth.

After a quick bath, we went out to enjoy a lovely Devon cream tea in the Park Café – not far from the Manor Hotel, where we were staying. It was an excellent cream tea served on a wooden platter, sprinkled with icing sugar – scones and little pots of clotted cream and jam.

After the three-course evening meal at the Manor Hotel, we went to join the crowds watching the Exmouth floodlit carnival until 9.30 p.m. Returning to the hotel, we enjoyed a lovely iced birthday cake baked by Gaynor (a fruit cake plus plenty of brandy), decorated in mauve and white with the words 'Happy Birthday Everyone!' Mel and John had provided two bottles of champagne (those were the only two not celebrating a special birthday). So a big thank you to everyone for the laughter and good time we all had.

The red cliffs between Exmouth and Budleigh Salterton with the curve of the mouth of the River Otter.

Budleigh Salterton to Sidmouth

Distance: 6.9 miles
Weather: sunny
Grade: moderate then strenuous

The path ahead along the shingle beach of Budleigh Salterton looked tantalisingly close, except the path went inland instead for a detour in order to cross the River Otter. Once again I was walking on my own.

The area on each side of the path is a haven for birds, and noticeboards displayed pictures of what birds might be seen. The path reached a lane and here I had to turn right over a bridge, following the lane before turning right towards the coast, bordering a field of wheat almost in ear. A short distance on found me looking down over the curved river mouth, the pebbled beach and a car park.

It was a lovely day. Skylarks flew overhead as I continued my walk, first on a cliff edge and then edging fields of oats and barley. Then came several steep climbs. I remember this walk as much for the lovely views inland over the fertile agricultural land as for the lovely views along the coast.

There is an enormous caravan park at Ladram Bay. The red/ terracotta-coloured rock stacks, just offshore, are said to be over 250 million years old – they are the oldest rocks along the coast.

Then came the climb to the High Peak. The path passes a beautiful old thatched building (now the campsite pub) and shortly afterwards I saw a wooden bench-type seat with the words 'In memory of Joy – take a pew and admire the view'!

I did indeed admire the view. The memorial part was a bit premature for this Joy!

Not long before, a young man stopped to ask about my walk (having noticed all the badges on my rucksack). He told me he was in training to do the Three Peaks Challenge – Snowdon, Ben Nevis and Scafell Pike in twenty-four hours. He said this was good practice ground, and off he ran!

The path entered a small woodland before opening out to a more level area of woodland with fantastic purple foxgloves.

The Peak is just off the official coastal path, reached up a steep path with a beautiful view. Later, at the end of the wood, there was a lovely viewpoint, where I stopped to admire the red cliffs of Sidmouth.

The path reached a grassy area down a zigzag path, next to a white Jacob's Ladder, before reaching the main esplanade. There I phoned to be picked up. I always phoned at the end of my walks to save Cyril (my friend picking me up) having to find a parking place for his larger-than-mine camper van. It usually worked well, but there is always that one exception! On this occasion after waiting for about half an hour I received a phone call from him and the conversation went like this:

"I can't see you. Where are you?"

I replied, "I'm standing by the bright-green lorry."

"I can't see a bright-green lorry! Where are you in relation to the red car going up the hill?"

I replied, "I can't see a red car – or a hill!"

A brief pause.

"What town are you in?"

"Sidmouth," I replied.

Another brief pause.

"Oh, I'm in Seaton!"

Ten miles away!

Perhaps if it had been pouring with rain, or bitterly cold, I might not have seen the funny side of it, but I went off to buy an ice cream and we had a laugh over it afterwards.

My last three walks – Weston Mouth to Seaton, Sidmouth to Weston Mouth, and Seaton to Lyme Regis through the undercliff – were the last three walks I did before completing the whole 630 miles of the South West Coast Path, so they are described at the end of this book.

Meanwhile in 2015, when I was eighty, I wanted to do something to celebrate my eightieth year. I decided to walk the entire Dorset coast as that is approximately eighty miles.

THE DORSET COAST

Lyme Regis to Charmouth

Date: May 2015

I camped at a campsite at Seatown and caught a double-decker bus from nearby Chideock to Lyme Regis. As it was a lovely day, Lyme Regis was packed with holidaymakers.

I walked to the Cobb, at the harbour, and then to the far end of the car park, where the path to the Landslip Nature Reserve (the Devon/Dorset boundary) can be seen, and then returned to the Cobb.

The harbourside cottages and buildings are worth admiring, and the lamp posts have a fossil-shaped decoration (Lyme Regis being famous for its fossils). At the end of the esplanade is the main street, and one has to turn right. Unfortunately, due to the many landslides on this section of the coast, major diversions have had to be put in place, so leaving Lyme Regis was very tedious – at least for a mile, walking up to a steep A-road with traffic hurling by. Thankfully there was a pavement.

Later the coastal path diversion sign directed walkers across the golf course with the help of white markers on stones. The path later dropped down through a woodland carpeted with bluebells to reach the A3052. Turning right, I continued down the hill to the roundabout, and then along the road towards Charmouth, and shortly afterwards took the steps on the right to a stile and public footpath. Following the paths and lanes I eventually reached the narrow bridge over the River Char on the beach at Charmouth.

It was not a great distance walked, but – what with the traffic, road walking, etc. – enough for that day! After an ice cream, I caught the bus back to Chideock and walked three-quarters of a mile back to the campsite at Seatown.

The harbourside cottages at Lyme Regis. Note the lamp posts have fossil shaped-decoration, Lyme Regis being famous for its fossils.

Charmouth to Seatown

Weather: sunny

The next day I left the campsite at Seatown and headed towards Golden Cap. It was a lovely sunny day.

Walking westwards, I climbed to the trig point on Golden Cap (the highest cliff on the south coast of Britain). It is a very steep, sharp climb, possibly more than a mile, instead of the long-drawn-out west-to-east route, with Golden Cap always visible in the distance but never seeming to get closer! Eventually I got to the top! The views from the trig point at the top of Golden Cap on such a beautiful day were fantastic.

Seaward the hilly coastline seemed to sweep around almost in a semicircle, whilst inland the views were of geometrically-shaped fields, valleys, trees and herds of beef cattle with their calves and sheep grazing happily.

I descended down the other side of Golden Cap, down further steps, across pasture and later up another flight of steep steps with violets edging each step. At the top it opened on to an open grassed area, showing the coastline to Charmouth and beyond to Lyme Regis.

Below I could see the narrow bridge I had walked over the previous day at Charmouth.

As before, at Charmouth I caught the bus back to Chideock and walked the three-quarters of a mile back to the campsite at Seatown – a small hamlet with one pub and a vast caravan site.

The trig point at 627 feet (191 metres) on the top of Golden Cap, the highest point on the south coast, and the coastline beyond.

Seatown to Burton Bradstock

Weather: sunny

The following day I walked from the campsite at Seatown, down to the beach by the Anchor Pub, then turned eastwards up the very steep hill through a flock of grazing sheep. It was brilliant sunshine, and there was a brilliant blue sky.

I reached Thorncombe Beacon, one and a half miles from the site. Here again the views were far-reaching, hence the jubilee beacon basket set high on a pole.

The path dropped down to the small inlet at Eype Mouth and up the other side, backing on to another campsite, and then there was easy walking to West Bay – about three and a half miles. Reaching West Bay, with its small but busy harbour, I visited the little quayside church then climbed the surprisingly steep cliff path, which continued alongside a golf course.

There was more easy walking over downland grass with pink thrift flowers cascading over the yellow/golden sandstone cliffs.

The path then dropped down through a static caravan park, later turning inland for a short distance to cross over the stream and then returning to the cliff edge to continue to Burton Bradstock. There I left the coast path and walked down a lane to the main road to catch a bus back to Chideock and the three-quarters-of-a-mile lane back to the campsite. I was beginning to know that lane!

Looking back towards Lyme Regis, with the Thorncombe Beacon basket in the foreground.

Burton Bradstock to Abbotsbury Tropical Gardens

Weather: sunny

The following day I parked in the National Trust car park at Burton Bradstock and walked the coastal path via West Bexington to Abbotsbury Tropical Gardens. It was level walking, but very tiring along the Chesil Bank, where the pebbles steeply slope down to the water's edge.

The weather was beautiful.

I stopped for a coffee at the beach café at West Bexington before making the mistake of catching the bus back to my camper van. Why a mistake? It was a two-mile uphill road walk on a very hot day to reach the bus stop on the main road! Oh well, we can't win them all!

Eventually reaching my camper van, I then drove around and parked at Abbotsbury Tropical Gardens and walked back to West Bexington along mainly a concrete road, passing a small number of houses. On that stretch I saw a number of yellowhammers – the first I had seen for quite a while. Reaching West Bexington, where I had reached earlier in the day, I returned to the Abbotsbury Tropical Gardens, visiting the shop and the café.

With hindsight (that useless thing we all have!) it would have been easier if I had continued walking from West Bexington along the beach to Abbotsbury Tropical Gardens and caught the bus on the main road back to my camper van at Burton Bradstock.

Abbotsbury Tropical Gardens to West Fleet

I camped at the West Fleet campsite adjoining the Fleet. I drove my camper van to Abbotsbury village car park, and walked via the pretty village to the tropical gardens, visiting and photographing St Catherine's Chapel en route. Returning by the coastal path, I climbed the steep fields overlooking the swannery, seeing several pillboxes en route.

After walking past the swannery entrance, I climbed over two awkward stone stiles on to the hill. This walk is different from previous sections of the coastal path mainly because it goes more inland, running parallel to the sea, due to the nature reserve.

There were lovely views from the ridge. Then I walked along the edge of a winter-wheat field, then bordered a wood, then through meadows of wild flowers and then pasture fields where a herd of cattle was grazing.

I didn't meet any walkers the whole day – who said I couldn't be quiet!

I walked through a campsite to the main road and caught a bus back to Abbotsbury to reach my camper van and drove to my campsite.

That evening, after a meal I decided to walk through the rifle-range section of the path to make sure they weren't firing. Yes, they had taken down the red flag, which meant they weren't firing, but they had left the further gate locked! So muggins had to clamber over the seven-foot gate – fortunately the bars were horizontal and not vertical. I then made it a circular walk back to the campsite.

West Fleet to Ferrybridge

The next day I walked to Ferrybridge, having moved to Pebble Bank Campsite at Wyke Regis, still adjoining the Chesil Bank and also overlooking the causeway to Portland.

The Isle of Portland

Date: June
Distance: 13 miles
Weather: spectacular

I must admit I had not been looking forward to this walk, but I loved it! I had mistakenly thought it would be level and boring! I remember it for spectacular weather and the wild flowers. There were cloudless blue skies, but a brisk breeze gave the sea lovely white horses.

I drove to Portland and parked at the free car park adjoining the Olympic rings by the war memorial viewpoint next to the Harbour Heights Hotel. From the car park I walked north towards Castletown to take photographs overlooking the old naval dockyard. The path then led behind the walls and barbed-wire fence of HM Prison The Verne, then zigzagged down to the broad path (dismantled railway).

There were lovely sea views on the left-hand side and steep stone cliffs on the other side. There were a dozen or so climbers rock climbing.

The lovely Church Ope Cove was reached by a lot of steep rocky stone steps, but it was well worth it for the wild flowers bordering the twisting path through the rocky section. The path opened out through the many disused stone quarries before levelling out as I reached the red-and-white lighthouse at Portland Bill.

With such lovely weather there were many visitors at the Bill. However, the stiff breeze made the sea an incredible sight – deep blue with white horses. The boats out at sea were having a good ride (rather them than me!).

I later walked around the picturesque Pulpit Rock before starting back on the western side of Portland, with views of the Chesil Bank stretching away for much of the way. It was mainly downland grass and maybe not as pretty as the eastern side, but I felt the view of the whole length of Chesil Bank more than made up for it. I felt I had chosen the prettier way to walk around Portland.

Towards the end the coastline became very rocky. Because of several rockfalls the coastal path was closed and diverted through stone quarries before the path took me across the road nearer the Olympic Rings viewpoint, where I took a number of photographs of the Chesil Bank below and the Olympic Rings in the foreground.

The following day I parked in the same car park and walked

the boring bit! – the causeway between Portland and Ferrybridge and back again. I walked from the Olympic Rings car park, down through Fortuneswell along the Chesil Bank side of the road to Ferrybridge, visiting and having coffee in the Chesil Beach Visitor Centre en route, returning on the opposite pavement.

I watched young teenagers having sailing lessons in the bay. Passing Osprey Quay, and then from the old part of the town, the path climbed steeply up a gully, past the houses in Castletown until I reached the old prison and car park. My circuit of the Isle of Portland was now complete.

This view looking from east to west along the Chesil Bank is taken from Portland. The Chesil Bank is eighteen miles long. The Olympic Rings were put there to celebrate the London 2012 Summer Olympics.

Ferrybridge to Ringstead

I camped at the Rosewall Riding Stables Campsite, overlooking the sea and adjoining the coast path – what more does anyone want? I could leave my camper van on site and did not to have to pay expensive car-parking fees (for example, the Smugglers Inn car park charged £5 for three hours; £10 for over three hours!).

Walking down through the campsite I joined the coast path and walked westwards towards Weymouth. The first thing I saw were the eighty-plus Friesian cows from the dairy adjoining the campsite.

There were fantastic views all along the coast around Weymouth Bay towards Portland. The path followed the coast in places, and went across fields before reaching the road at Bowlease Cove and then running along the long promenade to Weymouth.

Nearing Weymouth, the beach was very crowded. Opposite were pretty gardens, and one flower bed had been planted to commemorate the 100th anniversary of the WI. A Punch and Judy show surrounded by excited children was taking place on the beach. Opposite was a short street of decorative B & Bs with colourful flowers and flags.

I walked to the old harbour then followed the coast path up through a park before it opened out to a concrete path – a rather boring last mile before I reached the causeway at Ferrybridge, where I had finished on my last walk.

I was able to catch a frequent bus from Ferrybridge back to Weymouth seafront. I then walked down the long promenade to Bowlease Cove and back to the campsite. I then walked to, and returned from, Ringstead, walking by the Old Smuggler's Inn at Osmington Mills. It was an easy walk in perfect weather.

Loads of families were enjoying Ringstead Beach. I saw a lot of butterflies on bramble flowers, a few poppies, purple vetch and moon daisies.

Also on my walks in July, I saw a number of flat oblong beetles in a fascinating shiny bronze-green colour, which I hadn't seen before.

Ringstead to Durdle Door

Weather: sunny, but windy

I parked at the free National Trust car park above Ringstead, then walked across the fields past farm buildings to Ringstead Beach to join the coast path – later passing the old coastguard cottages at White Nothe. It was a lovely sunny day, but so windy. The gradients, both ascents and descents, were severe, particularly as I reached Durdle Door.

I think the Durdle Door section is one of the loveliest sections on the coastal path.

As I was making my way down the steep gradient just before Durdle Door, I was aware that a young couple, particularly the young man, was watching me with concern in case I slipped. Reaching the bottom, they spoke to me. I love accents, but I said I didn't recognise theirs. They told me they were Russian, visiting the West Country for the first time. I mentioned that I was walking the eighty-plus miles of the Dorset coast to celebrate my eightieth birthday.

He asked, "Do you mean an 8 and an 0? Please can we take a photograph of you?"

He then offered to take a photograph of me with my camera. I have met such friendly people on my walks.

Durdle Door to Bindon Hill

Date: April
Weather: sunny

I did this walk on a day trip from home.

I parked at Lulworth Cove main car park (£8 in total) and walked westward to Durdle Door up the steep wide paved pathway to just beyond the iconic Durdle Door and up the steep downland of Swyne Head, just beyond the sign to Scratchy Bottom. (Who thinks up these names?)

It was a beautiful day, the sun dazzling on the sea, with Portland and the causeway in the background. I took a number of photographs of the Durdle Door archway, then I returned to Lulworth Cove and walked around to Stair Hole, admiring the vertical and folded strata on the horseshoe-shaped Lulworth Cove.

The steep paths down the chalk downland just before Durdle Door.

Me photographed in front of the arch of Durdle Door.

Due to rockfalls, the path steps were closed, so I had to walk to the end of the village to take the steep path towards Bindon Hill. Then I cut back towards the edge of the cove (at low tide I believe it is possible to walk along the beach).

Spectacular views, spectacular weather – especially for April! Deep-blue sea, cloudless blue sky, sunshine, skylarks singing above, cowslips and golden gorse in bloom – what more could I wish for?

I headed for the Fossil Forest and spent some time photographing both the fossils and the deep-blue sea before climbing back up to continue along the path above the Fossil Forest to reach the beautiful Mupe Bay. Its steep white cliffs and rocky shore contrasted with the deep-blue sea and golden gorse bushes nearby.

Then came the steep, steep climb up to the top of the ridge of Bindon/Radar Hill (I think I counted 331 steps). At the top I saw the Army Memorial Stone and the carpet of cowslips. There I turned and made my way back to my camper van.

The Fossil Forest. It was nice to find something older than me on the walk!

Bindon Hill to Kimmeridge

Weather: changeable

This was a day trip on bank holiday Monday.

As it was a bank holiday, I knew the army ranges would be open for walking. I parked above Tyneham at Whiteway Viewpoint, but with hindsight it would have been better if I had parked in the actual village of Tyneham.

I walked along the ridge, reaching Flowers Barrow, then down a steep hill overlooking the military tanks used for shooting practice at Bovington to the beach at Arish Mell. There were two picnic tables and seats there, so I was able to rest before the task ahead – the steep, steep hill going towards Bindon Hill above Mupe Bay to reach the point where I left off on my previous walk. At the top I turned around and descended the same steep hill again, to return to Flowers Barrow! There I turned right, off the ridge, to follow the coast path down another steep hill above Worborrow Tout. Then I followed the ridge above Tyneham across sloping fields to Kimmeridge.

I walked by the Nodding Donkey Oil Wells, to reach the car park overlooking the bay. At that point I turned to walk back to my camper van – nearly two hours' walk away. It was at that point trouble started! It started to rain – no! More correctly, it began to lash down! And me without a coat! Well, it had been a lovely day when I set out! I had forgotten the golden rule: never go without a coat! (This walk was undertaken three years before my experience at Dodman Point.) I was soaked. The muddy track down to Tyneham was lethal, then I had to walk through the ruined village and up another muddy slippery chalky track to reach my camper van. Oh, how I wished I had parked down in Tyneham village!

Kimmeridge to Chapman's Cove

Distance: 4 miles

I parked at Kimmeridge car park, overlooking the beach.

On the way to the Clavell Tower on the clifftop I noticed the blackthorn was still out. After going up the cliff steps I stopped to read the noticeboard about the history of the Clavell Tower. It had been moved further back from the cliff edge in 2007–08 to safeguard it from falling into the sea. I was also surprised to read it could be rented out – no doubt at a high price.

There were lovely views, both coastal and inland, to Swyne Head, with fields of yellow rape and larks singing overhead.

Most of the walk was across open downland except one deep valley through woodland with wild garlic and one steep flight of 171 steps down to the cliff above Chapman's Cove. I descended only to turn at that point and climb back up the same 171 steps, to return to my camper van at Kimmeridge – four miles there and four miles back.

Chapman's Cove to Dancing Ledge

I parked at Worth Matravers – one of my favourite villages – and walked through the village and across fields to join the coastal path at the point where I left it the day before, in the deep valley at Chapman's Pool.

Near Kingston I passed the Royal Marines memorial and garden, dedicated to those who had lost their lives since World War Two. On the memorial is written, 'Rest awhile and reflect that we who are living can enjoy the beauty of the sea and countryside.' How true!

The path continued over downland, and I had to negotiate 122 steps down followed by 215 very steep steps up to reach a concrete seat put there to admire the view.

On the headland is a row of coastguard cottages, the square-built St Aldheim's Chapel and a lookout. Nearby a circular metal memorial commemorates the work carried out in that area on radar.

From here there is an easy walk to Winspit and the now closed stone quarries, where stone was quarried for centuries and loaded on to boats anchored at the foot of the cliffs. Stone quarried in that area was used to build most of London, including St Paul's Cathedral.

I continued to Seacombe and on to Dancing Ledge, which is very popular for rock climbing, caving and swimming in a natural pool carved out of the flat rock surface. I then took an inland route back to Worth Matravers and my camper van.

The poppies in bloom around the Royal Marines memorial, just off the South West Coast Path near Kingston.

Dancing Ledge to Swanage

Weather: sunny

In fact I walked from Swanage to Dancing Ledge and back to Swanage. It was a beautiful day.

Reaching Dancing Ledge, there were several groups of young people and their leaders dressed in caving gear and hard helmets and also some rock climbers and families picnicking.

Most of the walk after that was across open downland with glorious sea views. At the Lighthouse the path then went around to Tilly Whim Caves, and later a steep flight of wide stone steps led up to the Globe with Swanage Castle perched above it.

The path went seaward of the castle and then down through a wooded area – so cool on such a hot day. Eventually it led out on to an open grassed area with far-reaching views to Bournemouth and Boscombe and across the water to the Needles and the Isle of Wight.

I walked around to the old pier with all its ironwork, then around the beach to the far end.

Swanage to South Haven Point

Date: 17 October 2015
Weather: grey and chilly

I had officially left my walking friends at the Helford Estuary a few miles after the midway marker. I am delighted to say they continued and were walking this final section in October 2015 and they invited me to join them.

The walkers were Gaynor and Lionel, Mel, John, Jo, Kathy and myself. Jennifer joined us in the evening.

I had walked the entire Dorset coast (except on one day) with lovely blue skies, so it was a shame for this last section there were grey skies and there was quite a chill in the air – especially for Jo, who was wearing her usual shorts!

Leaving our cars at the end of the walk – South Haven Point by the ferry – we caught the open-top double-decker bus from the ferry to Swanage. At Swanage we walked to the seafront with our last cliff climb, Ballard Down, ahead of us. Walking the length of the seafront, we walked first up through residential roads and a chalet estate before reaching a grassed area high above the beach. Following the coast-path signs, we climbed up over Ballard Down, with glorious views both back to Swanage Bay and ahead towards Bournemouth with the Needles and the Isle of Wight in the distance.

The white chalk stacks of Old Harry Rocks looked beautiful, and after a stop to take photographs we continued through Studland, passing the Bankes Arms Public House. A signpost directed us back towards the beach, where we passed what at first looked like a straight wall, but on further examination I realised it was an unusual wartime pillbox. Nearby a memorial stone commemorates those lost in Studland Bay whilst practising for the D-Day landings.

Reaching the beach at Studland, we used the picnic tables for our last picnic together.

Then came the last stretch of beach – towards the winning post! This was a beautiful stretch of sandy beach, but due to recent storms there was some seaweed and, much to our surprise, masses of large pale-blue jellyfish as large as fancy wedding hats!

The long sandy beach, backed by sand dunes, finally curved around to the entrance of Poole Harbour and the blue metal marker erected to mark the end of the 630-mile South West Coast Path. Congratulations to all who had completed every mile of it – what a great achievement!

At this stage (October 2015) I had completed approximately 420 miles, of which I had walked 225 miles on my own. I was hopeful that in 2016 and beyond I would be able to complete some of the remaining 210 miles in South Devon and South Cornwall.

After returning to the hotel where we were staying – Norden House, just outside Corfe Castle – we showered and went out for a fabulous meal at the Castle Inn in Corfe. After this we returned to Norden House to open (you've guessed it) two bottles of champagne and cut a beautiful cake, made by Gaynor. (This has already been said previously.)

The celebration cake made by Gaynor, complete with walkers and rucksacks, coffee flask and a map of Devon, Cornwall and Dorset.

Walking along Studland Beach we were amazed to see how many jellyfish had been washed up on the beach following the recent storms. This one looked like a wedding hat! The glove gives an idea of the size of it.

THE LAST THREE WALKS OF MY 630-MILE WALK AROUND THE SOUTH WEST COAST PATH

Weston Mouth to Seaton

This section of coast path is described in the walk book as severe – and it is! Because the weather was in the mid to high twenties and I knew there were steps, steps and more steps, I decided to do this section in two halves – the latter part first, parking at the mile-inland Sidmouth Donkey Sanctuary to make it possible to do so. After being dropped off at the sanctuary I made my way downhill all the way to the beach at Weston Mouth. That mile-downhill bit seemed a good idea at the time, but I was forgetting that it would be all uphill to the sanctuary after I finished the walk back to Weston Mouth from Sidmouth (more about that later).

At Weston Mouth, the path only went for a few yards on the beach before turning inland again to climb steeply up over the cliffs. After a good level high stretch, the path eventually turned inland to meet a track and continue through woodland with occasional views to the village of Branscombe.

There were several lovely viewpoints from benches overlooking the spectacular coastline. The path descended to Branscombe Mouth, which was quite busy.

The path again climbed up steeply, and then two paths were possible. One of the paths led through a chalet park and then through an undercliff path between scrubland. However, I chose the higher path, which meant having first to climb up what I call a staircase to heaven – long steep straight steps with only a blue sky at the top! But it was worth it to look down on the undercliff path between scrubland and the spectacular cliffs.

The most unusual part of this walk was the dramatic red sandstone cliffs at one end and the white chalk cliffs at the other end. These are the most westerly chalk cliffs in England.

Both paths meet at the top of Beer Head.

The path then passes an inland caravan site and enters the village of Beer, dropping downhill on a road to the attractive beach, passing a row of attractive cottages. The path continues on the east side of the beach by climbing up steeply to the clifftop. It later descends to a road at Seaton Hole.

The path, when the tide is in, takes to the road, which eventually leads to the promenade, where I waited to be picked up.

Sidmouth to Weston Mouth

Weather: sunny

This was my last walk on my own before my friends joined me for the very last section of the whole walk!

I started my walk early as the weather was forecast to be hot – as it turned out to be. It was a lovely morning as I walked along the seafront of Sidmouth, before crossing the bridge and winding my way up through the narrow lanes to eventually go diagonally across a lovely steep meadow filled with summer flowers with butterflies dancing among them.

The view back along the coast was outstanding with its red cliffs, cloudless blue sky and even darker-blue sea – the coastline I had already walked disappearing into the distance.

What followed were steps, steps and more steps! Some zigzagged up steep cliffs; some went straight up through open areas and small woodland. One of these open areas had a wonderful panoramic view over Weston Mouth and well beyond.

I met some lovely people whilst walking that path, passing

A staircase to heaven? The many steps to reach the top of Beer Head.

One of my favourite views of both red sandstone and chalk cliffs between Sidmouth and Seaton.

when one or other of us had stopped to take a breather. I stopped to talk to an American family on the beach when I reached Weston Mouth before I started the long haul up to the donkey sanctuary, and halfway up with only another half a mile to go I remember thinking, 'I wish there was some shade here, but I think I'll sit down anyway.' At that moment apparently I fainted, and I came to to find the American family that had spoken to me on the beach looking after me. They helped me up and carried my rucksack and walked with me to the donkey sanctuary, where I was being picked up. In fact, my lift was already there waiting for me on that occasion! I think perhaps my fainting may have been due to several things; it was too hot, there were too many steps and just before that I had been stung by a horsefly (or should that be called a donkeyfly?!). However, on a positive note, having walked over 600 miles in total with only two falls (tripping over tufts of grass) and my one faint, that ain't bad at nearly eighty-four!

The steps leading down to Weston Mouth near Sidmouth Donkey Sanctuary.

Seaton to Lyme Regis

Weather: wet

Before I describe the last section of my walk I will write about the famous landslip between Seaton and Lyme Regis.

This is the nearest thing, they say, to a virgin forest that Britain has – caused by a landslip over Christmas 1839. It had been an excessively wet autumn, and rainfall had, it seems, permeated the clifftop layers of porous chalk and greensand which lay on clay, tilted towards the sea. Eight-million tons of waterlogged chalk and acres of fields slipped forward, forming gaping chasms and isolated rock stacks. The entire area – bearing in mind that it is about six miles in length – has been left to recover and develop without man's intervention. It was designated a National Nature Reserve in 1955/56.

I will also give a description of the weather on the day we walked that section.

It rained and rained and rained and rained,
The average fall was well maintained
And when the tracks were simply bogs
It started raining cats and dogs.

After a drought of half an hour
We had a most refreshing shower
And then the most curious thing of all –
A gentle rain began to fall.

Next day was also fairly dry
Save for the deluge from the sky,
Which wetted the party to the skin;
After that the rain set in!

Anon

The steps down into the famous undercliff.

Walking through the famous undercliff between Seaton and Lyme Regis
– an area of 800 acres and stretching nearly six miles.

I would like to be able to say that I wrote that myself, but I brought the poem back after walking in the rainforests in New Zealand many years ago. I love the way New Zealanders refer to walking as tramping.

The original group of walkers who started at the Yarn Market Hotel – Kathy, Mel, Jo, Gaynor and Lionel – joined me to finish this very last section of the 630 miles of the South West Coast Path. Walking from our hotel in Seaton, we stopped for a group photograph at the start of the walk, where sadly Gaynor had to leave us due to back problems which she had recently been suffering from.

It was already raining at that point. We climbed up a track to reach the golf course and a viewpoint known as Goat Island. A large noticeboard warned us that there was no escape route once we had started walking.

After a grassy area the path descended through woodland to enter the dense world of the undercliff – often described as quite eerie! Except for about a mile at the further end, near Lyme Regis, the path is a narrow one which twists and turns without sight of sea or sky, because of the tree canopy. It dips over wooden bridges and climbs through the nearest thing in England to an Amazon rainforest. On that day the emphasis was on the word *rain* – we were drenched!

The path was muddy and very slippery, with exposed tree roots and exposed chalk and flints.

I would have liked to have looked around more at the trees and rock foundations, but our eyes had to be kept looking down at where we were walking for safety reasons, and a lot of photographs were wasted due to condensation on my camera lens, or my glasses!

The path twisted and turned throughout, among trees, tangles of creepers and ferns, and we could see a new cliff line to our left in one place.

We passed a number of fingerposts saying 'Lyme Regis', but strangely none gave the mileage, which was rather disheartening in such bad weather. In just one place we glimpsed the sea!

Eventually we began to see the sky and reached a lane before diagonally crossing an open area. Then we followed a series of steps down into a car park near the Cobb at Lyme Regis.

At some stage we had crossed the border between Devon and Dorset.

As we walked along the Cobb, the sea was rough and grey. We made our way to a café to have a hot drink and a cream tea or cake. We had to apologise to the café owner for the puddles we had made on the floor because of our drenched coats, but he politely told us not to worry, as did the taxi driver who drove us back to our hotel in Seaton with towels and newspapers draped over the seats.

It's amazing how a long soak in a hot bath can revive cold, tired walkers!

We had our evening meal at the hotel and afterwards Gaynor invited us to their room for a surprise celebration. Gaynor had made and decorated a lovely fruit cake with the words 'Well Done Joy. South West Coast Path', and it was decorated with cake fossils. And needless to say we celebrated in the usual way – opening two bottles of champagne. They also gave me a congratulations card signed by them all.

As Cyril had helped me so much with transport on my walks, he was also invited to the meal and celebration. A few days later I also received a congratulations card from Trish and Malcolm (Trish having walked three of the walks with me). It was a home-made card. On the front it had a photograph of me taken about seventy years previously, after a deckchair had given way underneath me!

I am left wondering how many more photographs like that she has of me.

After our day of walking the undercliff in such torrential rain, my walking friends gave me a wall plaque which reads, 'Life isn't about waiting for the storm to pass – it's about learning to dance in the rain!' Good advice for life!

Having completed the entire 630 miles (1,014 km) of the South West Coast Path, I am both glad and sad. It is satisfying to complete a task that I have set myself, but it is also sad because

I have so enjoyed walking this fabulous coast – in spite of all the steps, the torrential rain on occasions and the intense heat on others! According to the *South West Coast Path Book* there are over 30,000 steps.

Even now, looking back, I can remember vividly the occasions when I felt so content and almost overwhelmed by the sheer beauty of the scenery – so many places which only walkers see! It also made me appreciate how blessed I was, to be still able to walk and enjoy our beautiful coastline at the age of nearly eighty-four. To the glory of God! I wouldn't have missed doing this walk for all the world!

I have met so many lovely people en route, but in particular I am grateful for my lovely bunch of friends, who were all strangers when we started out on our lovely venture of walking the South West Coast Path!

South West
Coast Path
Association

Joy Gower
WALKED THE SOUTH WEST COAST PATH
BRITAIN'S LONGEST NATIONAL TRAIL (630 MILES)